D1615817

Miniature Trees in the Japanese Style

Pinus parviflora in the Winding style. Stones have been used carefully to give a natural effect

MINIATURE TREES IN THE JAPANESE STYLE

Gillian E. Severn

N. D. H.

with line drawings by Irene Hawkins

TAPLINGER PUBLISHING COMPANY

NEW YORK

First Published in the United States in 1968 by
TAPLINGER PUBLISHING CO., INC.
29 East Tenth Street
New York, New York 10003

Library of Congress Catalogue Card Number
68–10987

Printed in Great Britain

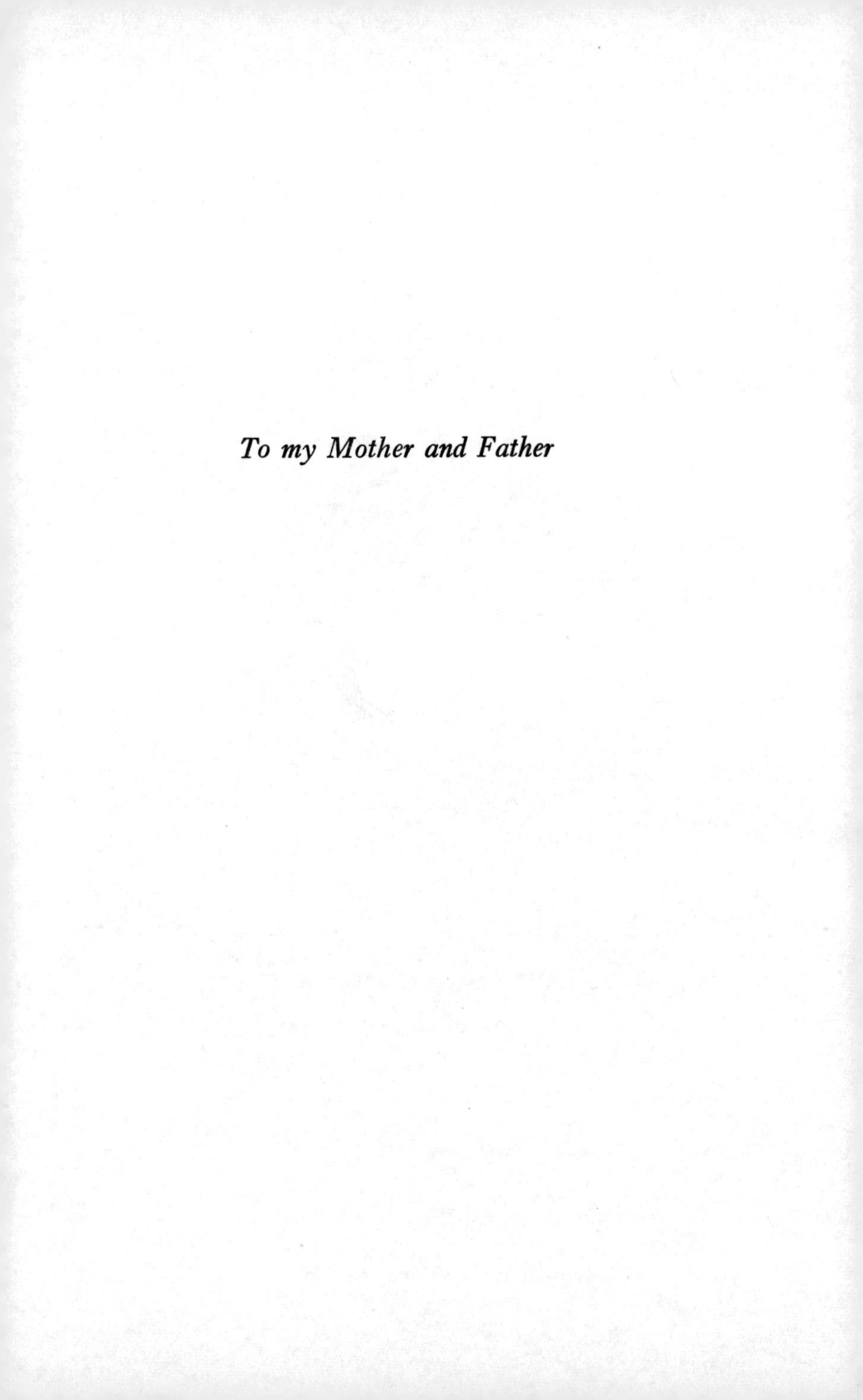

To my Mother and Father

Little Fellows

The Japanese
Grow tiny trees
About so high!
I wonder why

Reginald Arkell

Acknowledgements

I would like to thank a number of people for the help and encouragement that they have given me while preparing this book: Mr. Lawrence Hills read the manuscript and gave some welcome advice; Mr. J. E. Downward took all the photographs, including the frontispiece, except Plate 16 which was taken by my husband; Miss Irene Hawkins very kindly agreed to make the line drawings based on my original sketches.

Grateful acknowledgement is made to Herbert Jenkins Ltd. for permission to reproduce the poem 'Little Fellows' from *Collected Green Fingers* by Reginald Arkell.

My special thanks go to my husband who read and typed the manuscript several times with great patience.

GILLIAN SEVERN
West Downs Pike, Winchester, 1967

Contents

List of Illustrations

PLATES

LINE DRAWINGS IN THE TEXT

A ten-year-old *Fagus sylvatica* (Beech) grown in the Upright style, showing a method of curling the long young shoots. Note the off-centre planting

Introduction

This book is not intended to be a detailed account of the history and art of bonsai growing. Instead, the author has tried to provide a simple and practical guide for anyone who wants to make a start. In articles and books published previously we can find quite extensive details of how bonsai are grown in their original home, Japan. These details include descriptions of Japanese soils and manures, but in the following pages the information given is related to what is available in our nurseries and garden-centres at the present time in the way of containers, soils, manures, and so on.

There is a growing interest in these fascinating trees and they can be displayed in a number of places—living-rooms, conservatories, terraces, verandas and even kitchen window-sills. In fact, the window-sill is an admirable place for those that are being trained or those that are not being displayed. There is nothing to prevent flat-dwellers from taking up the 'art', just as they have been growing 'house plants' in profusion for the past few years. Bonsai are even better suited to cultivation in the average British rooms than a great many house plants that people struggle to grow. The expert Japanese bonsai grower Kyozo Morata once said, 'Like a pet animal, it needs water, sunshine and nourishment.'

The names used are based on those used in *Trees and Shrubs Hardy in the British Isles*, by W. J. Bean.

Any lists given are not complete, but are intended to serve as guides for those wishing to start a collection.

Abbreviations used in Chapter 2

br. = branches
fl. = flowers
fr. = fruit
l. = leaves
var. = variety

I
What is Bonsai?

Bonsai have been grown in Japan for hundreds of years and their culture is a treasured art which has been passed on from generation to generation. There are, in Japan, a number of bonsai specimens which are known to be more than a hundred years old and these are, of course, of very considerable value. One plant is believed to be a thousand years old. This does not mean, however, that one has to wait all that time for them to grow. The thousand-year-old specimen was probably looking a shapely and venerable tree at the time of the Norman Conquest when it was a hundred years old, and the centenarian trees were small and decorative by their third year. The species used are not special dwarf ones, but quite ordinary trees and shrubs, only some of which come from Japan; they are plants which would attain considerable heights when grown unchecked, and ones which anyone can grow from seeds or cuttings and dwarf by the methods described in this book.

As a rough guide, the age to which a bonsai may grow should correspond to that of a tree growing naturally; in fact, it will often exceed it because the bonsai is given such care and attention, never having to contend with the extremes of nature. As a rule conifers live longer than deciduous trees and deciduous forest trees outlive ornamental flowering trees and shrubs.

In the bonsai circles of Japan a thirty-year-old bonsai is looked on as mature, but full beauty cannot be expected in less than fifty years. However, this should not discourage beginners who will take heart as soon as they have their first specimen, even if it is only a year or so old or a newly potted seedling.

Before setting out to grow bonsai, we must define the meaning of the word 'bonsai'. It is made up of two Japanese words —'bon' meaning a shallow pan, and 'sai' meaning a plant. By being planted in shallow containers trees can be greatly dwarfed, but not necessarily starved. The object of all the care and effort in bonsai culture is to dwarf the stem, shoots and leaves of each specimen in order to achieve, finally, a well-proportioned miniature. They have sometimes been referred to as 'those poor little underfed trees in tiny pots'. This idea is quite unfounded as will be seen from Chapter 6. Bonsai are, in fact, pot-grown miniature replicas of their natural counterparts in the wild; they may be beautifully shaped, upright specimens or gnarled, twisted curiosities, and may be grown singly or in groups. In height they vary from two inches to as much as three feet.

In Japanese homes, including the most humble, bonsai are given a place of honour in the main room. As readers will know, the furniture and furnishings of a Japanese house are kept very simple, but owners always try to have a miniature tree indoors throughout the year. To do this they have a collection of trees, coniferous and deciduous, from which to choose. The plants grown are hardy and thrive best if they can be 'rested' in the open for quite long periods of time. This 'rest' is good for their health and helps to widen the interest for the grower, as he does not have the same plant (or plants) in the house all the time, which is the case with too many house plants. When the bonsai are put in the open, the containers may be plunged to their tops in sand or soil, or arranged on a table, terrace or veranda. The plunging method helps to prevent the soil drying out quite so quickly in very hot weather, and hence cuts down the amount of watering neces-

This Oblique *Pinus parviflora* is rather spoilt by clumsy wiring. Note use of moss

sary. In winter, however, it would be unwise to decide to put a bonsai out in the open in frosty spells, since the sudden change of temperature, from warmth to cold, could cause the leaves to wilt or fall; the containers also are likely to be damaged by the action of frost. If available, a cold greenhouse would be an excellent place for 'resting' plants in winter.

The species and varieties grown for bonsai are selected for the interest they offer in one or more of the following: shape, leaf-colour, flower and fruit. The list that follows includes some of the easiest species to grow and is intended to give the reader some ideas upon which to build his bonsai collection.

SIMPLIFIED LIST OF SUITABLE SUBJECTS FOR BONSAI WORK

Grown on account of interesting shapes

Acer—for leaf shape and natural shape of tree
Conifers
Quercus (Oak)
Weeping willow

Grown for leaf colour

Acer
Berberis thunbergii 'Atropurpurea'
Conifers
Ginkgo biloba
Taxodium distichum (Bald Cypress)

Grown for flowers

Azaleas
Chaenomeles lagenaria (*Cydonia japonica*)
Forsythia
Jasminum nudiflorum
Malus sp.

Grown for flowers (*continued*)
Prunus sp.
Tamarix juniperina (Tamarisk)

Grown for fruit
Cotoneaster
Crataegus
Ilex (Holly)
Malus sp.

More details of these plants are given in Chapter 2, where the different styles are described.

In this country, as mentioned above, bonsai could well take the place of pot-plants and in general have the same requirements; for example, they need good light and careful watering and feeding. With regard to temperature they are not so exacting—they are hardy and will stand frost provided that they are not suddenly subjected to it after having been in a moderately heated living-room. These hardy plants do not, in fact, like high temperatures and they should be kept away from hot radiators. In these days when more and more central heating is being fitted, it is the hot radiators that are more likely than anything else to cause damage to bonsai in the winter. Good light is one of the main essentials for healthy and even growth, and for this reason the nearer they can be put to the window the better. The best light value will naturally be at the window, and if bonsai are placed on the window-sill, they should be turned round once daily to prevent uneven growth, as plants always grow towards the source of light. But it should be remembered that in very hot weather serious scorching can occur through glass; so at such times bonsai should not be left in the window—they will need to be moved to a shadier part of the room or, better still, placed out of doors where they will not scorch.

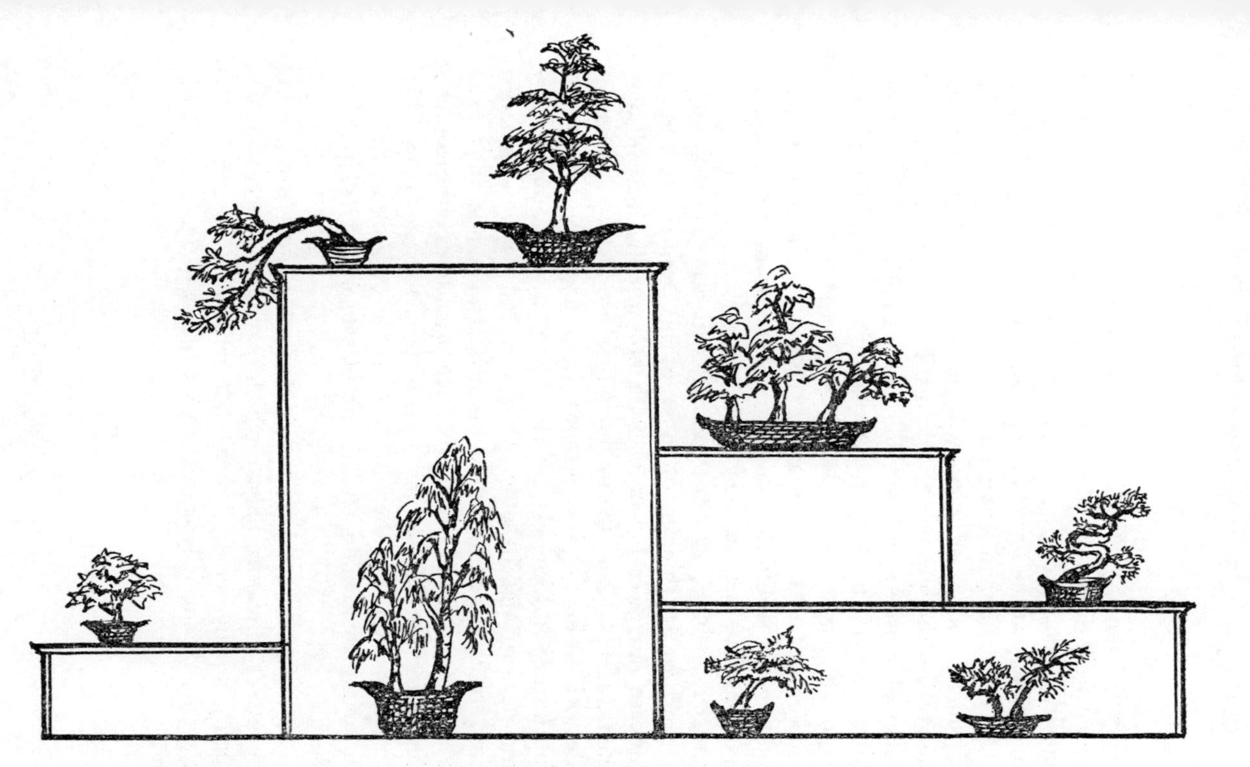

1. A specially constructed stand for the display of a collection of mame bonsai (see p. 24)

Apart from the fact that the light is best in the window, a window-sill does not make a good display place as there is not usually a good background against which the beauty of shape and colour can be seen to their best advantage. A plain background is ideal and its colour should be governed by the individual bonsai; evergreens will show up best against a pale colour, but the question of colour will naturally be a matter of personal opinion; green would of course not be a good choice. If the bonsai is to be appreciated at night, it should be placed, if possible, near a suitable light. A bonsai enthusiast might even go so far as to have a corner specially wired for hidden lighting. It would not be wise, however, to create a very 'Japanese' corner, as this could possibly stand out *against* rather than blend *with* the room and its other furnishings.

Since we are thinking of bonsai in this country, we will not concern ourselves too much with how the Japanese display theirs, except where the methods they use fit into our way of life without looking incongruous. In order to appreciate their full beauty and interest one should show bonsai individually and not crowded by other pot-plants and flowers. In Japan they are displayed on simple but attractive stands, the legs of which vary in height from one inch or so to several feet, and depending on the size and style of tree, they are placed low down or high up; the beauty of some bonsai, particularly those in the cascading style, is often best seen by looking up at them.

If ordinary bonsai are considered too large, we can grow mame, or miniature bonsai, which may be only a few inches high (see Chapter 9). A very wide range of these can be displayed on a specially constructed stand (Fig. 1).

2
Classification and Suitable Subjects

Bonsai are grouped or classified in two ways, first by the shape of the trunk and secondly by the number of trees in a container. Details of the training necessary will be given in Chapter 5.

A. SHAPE OF TRUNK

UPRIGHT OR CHOKKAN STYLE

Trees in this style are grown as single specimens with a straight and upright trunk. They have a dignified appearance, just as a carefully tended specimen may have in a sheltered garden, or one that has grown in the wild, unmolested by wind or other unfavourable agents. The branches are trained to give pyramidal and columnar shapes to the head of the tree. There is a slightly less severe form in which the main trunk leans very slightly to one side or the other. Anything more than a very *slight* inclination would bring it into the next style—the Oblique. This style is the easiest to follow for beginners and pleasing results may be obtained quite quickly, as some species grow naturally in this shape. It should be noted here, however, that miniature species, often used in rock gardens, are not really suitable for bonsai work even after careful thinning, as their branches are formed too close together on the stem. This gives a crowded and cramped appearance quite out of keeping with the dignity and grace associated with a well-trained bonsai. (Fig 2)

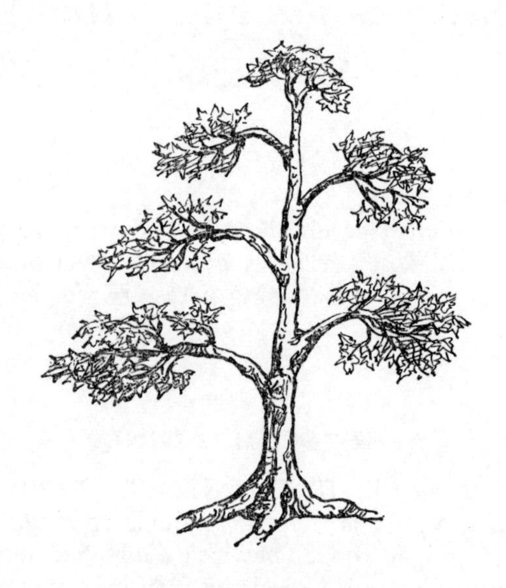

2. Upright or Chokkan style

SUITABLE SUBJECTS

DECIDUOUS

Acer palmatum Japanese Maple. Spreading, mushroom-shaped tree, 'cut' l.; good autumn colour.
Acer palmatum dissectum More finely cut.
Acer pseudoplatanus Sycamore.
Betula alba Silver Birch. Peeling, silvery bark.

Carpinus betulus Common Hornbeam. Naturally pyramidal shape, neat ovate l., veins deeply impressed, hop-like fruiting catkins.

Carpinus japonica Smaller tree with more conspicuous leaf-veins.

Crataegus oxycantha Common Hawthorn. L. oblong and lobed, dark glossy green; white fl. in May produced in clusters, followed by round, dark red berries.

Crataegus oxycantha 'coccinea plena' A double red form.

Fagus sylvatica Common Beech. Neat oval l., fresh bright green in summer; bronze autumn l. remain till spring.

Ginkgo biloba Maidenhair Tree. Pyramidal tree, fan-shaped l. which turn clear butter-yellow in autumn. One of the few deciduous conifers.

Quercus dentata Daimyo Oak. Very large, lobed l. remain through winter. Rare in this country.

Quercus myrsinaeflora Evergreen, narrow l. are purple-red when young.

Quercus robur Common Oak. This and its var. *cristata* are deeply lobed and curled forms.

Quercus serrata Small bright green l., clinging till very late autumn.

Taxodium distichum Bald Cypress. Feathery foliage, bright green in spring, dying off a rich brown; interesting knobbly roots at ground level. Another of the few deciduous conifers.

Zelkova serrata Japanese grey-bark Elm. Closely resembles the Common Elm l. narrow, ovate, serrated. Forms a broom-shaped tree.

EVERGREEN

Cedrus atlantica Atlas Cedar. Pyramidal when young with arching leader, forming a flattened top with age.

Cedrus atlantica glauca A glaucous form of the above.

Cedrus deodar Deodar. Tips of young shoots pendulous and downy.

Chamaecyparis pisifera plumosa Pyramidal in shape. L. feathery and of juvenile type, greyish-green.

Chamaecyparis pisifera squarrosa An even more feathery form and bluer in colour than *plumosa*.

Chamaecyparis obtusa L. rich green. Slow growing umbrella-shaped tree.

Cryptomeria japonica elegans L. curved, pointed and brownish green; bark peels off in narrow strips.

Juniperus chinensis Chinese Juniper. Slender, pyramidal shape.

Juniperus chinensis sargentii A prostrate form with bright green juvenile and glaucous adult l.

Juniperus procumbens Spreading habit. L. glaucous.

Picea excelsa Common Spruce. Naturally an upright, pyramidal tree; deep glossy green.

Picea jezoensis Yedo Spruce. Used greatly in Japan, but not easily grown in Britain.

Pinus densiflora Japanese Red Pine. Name taken from red bark. Dark green twisted l. arranged in pairs; young shoots slightly glaucous.

Pinus parviflora Japanese White Pine. L. arranged in fives and silvery underneath; young shoots downy. Believed to be the 'Pine' of the 'Willow Tree' pattern.

Pinus sylvestris Scots Pine. Red tinged-flaking bark.

Pinus thunbergii Black Pine. L. in pairs; bark on young shoots yellow-brown, darkening with age to almost black.

Taxus baccata Yew. L. dark glossy green, long and narrow, half an inch to one inch long. Separate male and female plants needed if red fleshy berries of quarter inch are wanted. Fl. insignificant.

Pinus parviflora grown in the Gnarled style

OBLIQUE OR SHAKAN STYLE

Trees of this style have an oblique trunk as if they had been growing in a windswept situation; consequently they tend to be more heavily branched on one side than the other. (Fig. 3)

3. Oblique or Shakan style

SUITABLE SUBJECTS

DECIDUOUS

Acer palmatum Japanese Maple. See page 26.

Acer palmatum dissectum See page 26.

Acer pseudoplatanus See page 26.

Forsythia suspensa Has a natural weeping habit; clear yellow fl. in clusters of two to six in March and April; l. oblong and slightly toothed.

Malus Crab Apple. Double season of interest—fl. in spring and fr. in autumn.

Malus floribunda Pale pink fl. in April; arching graceful br.; narrow l.; yellow fr.

Malus sieboldii Semi-weeping habit; fl. pale pink fading to white and smaller than last species; reddish-yellow pea-sized fr.

Prunus amygdalus Almond. Pale pink fl. in March; easily raised from suckers or cuttings.

Prunus incisa Fuji or Cut-leaved Cherry. Abundant white fl. in March; l. deeply toothed.

Prunus persica Peach. Pale rose fl. in April.

Prunus subhirtella Very pale pink fl. from mid-March onwards; easily raised from semi-ripe shoots in mid-summer.

Salix babylonica Weeping Willow. L. are lanceolate; female tree has two-inch-long catkins; bright yellow bark on young shoots.

Tamarix juniperina Tamarisk. L. very small and pointed; hundreds of minute pale pink fl. in May. May be damaged by severe frost, some protection will be needed.

EVERGREEN

Ilex aquifolium Common Holly. Dark green, glossy, toothed, prickly l., followed by bright red berries. There are many other forms of variegated hollies.

Picea excelsa Common Spruce—'Christmas Tree'. Has a naturally pyramidal form.

WINDING OR KYOKKUK STYLE

This style has a single but twisted trunk and represents the plant that has fought for its existence in the wild. The branches may also be twisted. The twisting of the trunk, apart from being interesting to look at, has a valuable dwarfing effect and can be useful if the material being trained has grown too tall and is still young and supple enough to be twisted. (Fig 4)

4. Winding or Kyokkuk style

SUITABLE SUBJECTS

DECIDUOUS

Azaleas Now included under Rhododendron. Any of the dwarfer forms are suitable, especially the Kurume group; fl. white, cream, pink, red, orange, mauve or purple in April-May. *R. obtusum* (magenta) and *R. serpyllifolium* (rose-pink), with tiny evergreen foliage.

Malus See page 29.

Salix babylonica See page 30.

EVERGREEN

Pinus parviflora See page 28.

Pinus sylvestris See page 28.

GNARLED OR HANKAN STYLE

This style is somewhat similar to the previous one, but the trunk grows closer to the soil and is knobbly and gnarled rather than merely twisted. This would represent a tree that has grown slowly in unfavourable conditions such as a poor and shallow soil in a windswept situation. Once again *Pinus parviflora* is one of the best types for training in this way and so is *P. sylvestris*. (Fig 5)

5. Gnarled or Hankan style

CASCADING OR KENGAI STYLE

As the name implies the trunk in this style cascades over the edge of the container as if it were hanging over a rock on a mountain side. It is important to choose a species with a relatively pliable stem. (Fig 6)

Pinus parviflora grown in the Gnarled style but not as attractive as plate 3 because more trunk is showing and the branches are not so well arranged

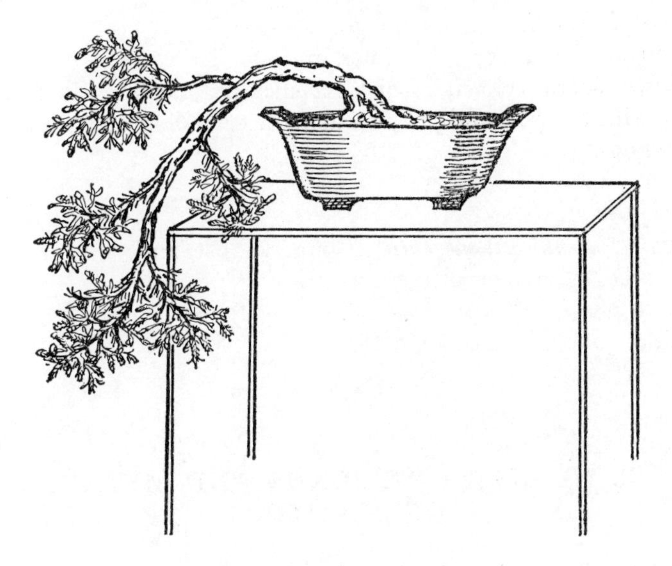

6. Cascading or Kengai style

SUITABLE SUBJECTS

DECIDUOUS

Chaenomeles lagenaria Quince. Possibly better known as *Cydonia japonica*. Cup-shaped fl. on a previous year's growth in March-April, followed by large quince fr.

Chaenomeles lagenaria 'Moerloesii' Pink and white.

Chaenomeles lagenaria 'Nivalis' White.

Chaenomeles lagenaria 'Rowallane Seedling' Blood red.

Cotoneaster horizontalis Fishbone Cotoneaster. Br. arranged as a fishbone; white fl. a quarter inch in diameter in May in small clusters, followed by small bright red berries remaining after l. The leaves colour well in shades of yellow, orange and red.

Salix babylonica See page 30.
Tamarix juniperina See page 30.
Wistaria brachybotris Long racemes of mauve fl. in May. Trim after flowering. Excellent in cascading and winding styles.

EVERGREEN

Juniperus chinensis sargentii Juniper. Prostrate form: juvenile l. light green, adult l. glaucous.
Pinus parviflora See page 28.
Pinus sylvestris See page 28.

B. NUMBER OF TRUNKS AND METHOD OF PLANTING

As well as being classified by the style in which they are trained, bonsai are classified further by means of the style of planting. They may be planted singly in a container or in threes and fives. The shape and character of the tree may be most fully appreciated if it is planted singly. The planting of more than one tree gives the effect of a miniature wood and so creates a different interest.

An odd number for planting is chosen not only because it has a more pleasing effect, but also because in Japan these numbers stand for age and immortality; both are greatly appreciated and respected.

IKADI-BUKI STYLE

Very often the trunk of a tree may be laid or trained horizontally and the branches of the upper side left to represent trees. (Fig 7)

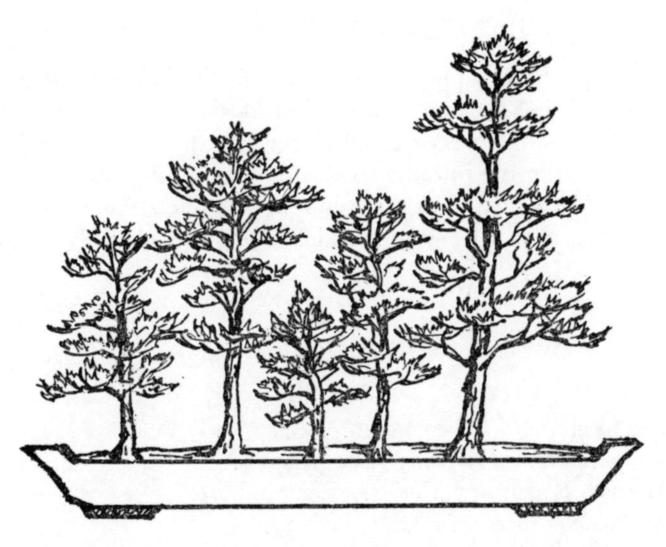

7. Single horizontal trunk trained in the Ikadi-buki style

SUITABLE SUBJECTS

DECIDUOUS

Acer palmatum See page 26.

Acer palmatum dissectum See page 26.

Chaenomeles See page 33.

Forsythia See page 29.

Ilex serrata A deciduous Japanese holly. L. oval and slightly toothed, downy when young, becoming shiny later; fr. round, red and remaining for a long time after leaf fall.

EVERGREEN

Cryptomeria japonica elegans See page 28.

Pinus parviflora See page 28.

Pinus sylvestris See page 28.

CLASPED TO STONE STYLE

This method of planting gives the feeling of age and tenacity which is so much in the mind of a Japanese bonsai enthusiast. A single tree is usually used and the roots are trained to cling and grow round a stone in a way similar to that often found on a windy, rocky mountain side. The stone itself may be set in a pan of water which adds considerably to the 'picture'.

SUITABLE SUBJECTS

DECIDUOUS

Acer palmatum See page 26.
Acer palmatum dissectum See page 26.
Azaleas Kurume varieties. See page 31.
Chaenomeles lagenaria See page 33.
Jasminum nudiflorum Winter Jasmine. Bright yellow, half inch to three quarter inch, fl. from Nov.–Feb., mainly Dec.–Jan.; l. oblong.

EVERGREEN

Juniperus chinensis sargentii See page 28.
Picea excelsa See page 28.
Pinus parviflora See page 28.
Pinus sylvestris See page 28.

Taxus baccata (Yew) grown in Clasped-to-Stone style; eighteen years old

3
How to Start

There are five main ways of raising young plants for bonsai:

1. Seed
2. Seedlings
3. Cuttings
4. Layering
5. Plants collected from the wild

In addition to these methods of obtaining a bonsai some firms are now supplying bonsai which have already had their initial training, and sometimes they are planted in suitable containers. They supply either British- or Japanese-grown plants. These 'ready-made' bonsai may or may not be entirely to the buyer's liking; if they are not they can, to a certain extent, be altered and improved by the new owner by judicious training and pruning. If the tree has not been planted in a way that pleases, this also can be adjusted when it is repotted.

Grafting and layering are also used in nurseries, but on the whole amateur bonsai growers would be well advised to content themselves with the other methods.

Each method is quite simple and may have advantages over the others, depending on the species concerned and whether or not large numbers are required.

1. SEED

One of the chief advantages of raising plants from seed is that large numbers can be obtained relatively cheaply. It is an interesting and rewarding method, especially if the seed has been collected by oneself. Seeds of conifers, beech, birch, *Chaenomeles* and many others can be collected quite simply, and there are seed firms that can supply seeds of a very wide range of species (see page 105). It should be remembered that the resulting seedlings often show variations and some may have to be discarded, but sometimes one may be fortunate enough to find a seedling that gives evidence of superior quality. Variations which may be detected at this early stage are usually only shown in leaf shape and colour. Thus if any seedlings have more attractive leaves they should be kept, whereas weak and unhealthy seedlings must be discarded.

Very hard-coated seeds, those of cherry, quince, *Chaenomeles*, beech, *Cotoneaster* and other Rosaceae species, yew, *Ginkgo*, *Ilex* and limes, germinate slowly and benefit from a

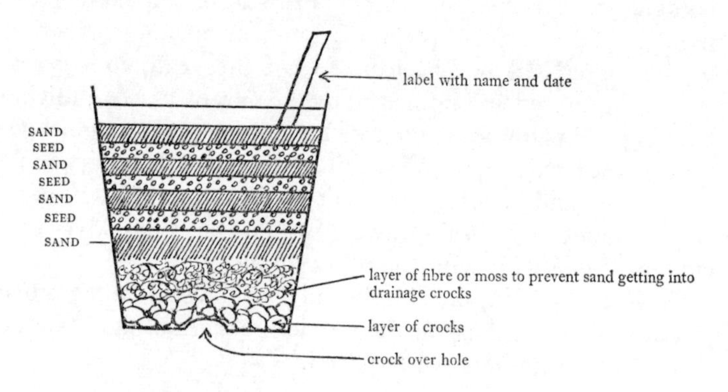

8. The stratification of hard-coated seeds in a 5-in. pot

process known as *stratification*. After collection or delivery the seeds are placed in layers in pots or boxes of sand, which are covered with wire-netting to keep birds and mice away, and put on a well-drained surface—ashes or clinkers—on the north side of a wall or hedge. Care should be taken to label the pots as it is easy to forget during the following months which seed was put in each pot (Fig. 8). They should be left for twelve to eighteen months and the more they are frozen the better; frost seems to help germination. Before sowing, usually in the spring, the seed may be sieved or washed free of sand and then sown in the orthodox way described below.

For sowing any seed the best receptacles are five-inch pots or seed pans, as these give good drainage and can be easily moved when necessary. The pot should be thoroughly cleaned and then 'crocked' and filled carefully. A large crock, convex side uppermost, is placed over the hole and covered with about an inch and a half of broken pot crocks or gravel, which in turn is covered with moss or fibre to keep the crocks free from soil (Fig. 9).

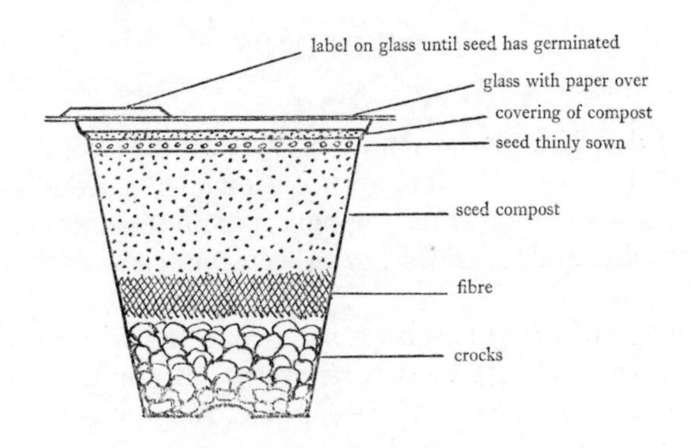

9. Seeds sown in 5-in. pot

John Innes Seed Compost is a good safe compost to use for all seeds, and each pot is filled and evenly firmed to within about half an inch of the top. This last rather depends on the size of the seed. Allow room to cover the seeds with their own depth of soil and leave a quarter-inch space for watering. This space is less at this stage than for later watering because the seedlings need to be as near the light as possible to prevent them from becoming 'drawn' and leggy.

The seed should be sown thinly, covered and then watered by plunging the pot to the rim in water until the water begins to appear at the surface. The pot is then covered with a sheet of glass and brown paper, and placed in a cold greenhouse, cold frame or on a window-sill. Turn the glass over each day to prevent condensation dripping on to the soil surface, and remove the paper as soon as the seedlings begin to appear. Water, when necessary, by plunging the pot as described above. The glass is increasingly raised on a label as the seedling leaves develop, and is finally removed altogether.

For the future treatment of the seedlings see Chapter 4.

2. SEEDLINGS

Town dwellers or owners of very small gardens may well not wish to use space for stratification and various pots of germinating seedlings. Starting bonsai from seedlings cuts out much trouble and, of course, can save as much as two years in time.

Seedlings of many species can be collected with very little difficulty, e.g. beech, sycamore, horse chestnut, holly and oaks, and less often some of the conifers. It is not generally the custom of nurseries in this country to supply very small seedlings, but by visiting the nursery personally it is sometimes possible to select what is wanted.

The best time to collect or select seedlings is in early spring just before they start into growth. When selecting, try to imagine the style and shape for which they are intended. Look not only at the trunk, but also at the branches or buds from which they will be formed. Above all choose a healthy plant, as it is unwise to pick out a small and possibly weak specimen, thinking that it will need less time spent on it to dwarf it. In order to ensure that selected seedlings grow on with little or no check, great care should be taken when digging them up. Use a trowel or small spade and lift the seedling with a good ball of soil round the roots. If the soil is at all dry, it would be worth giving it a good soak and waiting a few moments for the water to penetrate the soil. As soon as the seedling has been lifted the roots should be wrapped in a damp sack or, better still, strong polythene. If the seedling has to remain unpotted or unplanted for any length of time, after wrapping the roots the whole plant may be put in a polythene bag to conserve moisture in the leaves and so prevent wilting. Readers should pause before going in search of seedlings or wild plants as obviously in their eagerness to find suitable plants they must not go digging on private or public property without permission.

The following subjects may be raised from seed or seedlings (× denotes easier subjects):

DECIDUOUS

× *Acer*
× *Betula*
Carpinus
× *Cotoneaster*
Crataegus
× *Fagus*
Ginkgo
Ilex
Malus
Prunus
× *Quercus*
Taxodium
Zelkova

EVERGREEN

Abies
× *Cedrus*
Ilex
× *Picea*
× *Pinus* (leave seedlings in seed-pot for one year)
Taxus

3. CUTTINGS

Young plants can often be obtained more quickly by taking cuttings than by raising them from seed, and so for many subjects it is the best method to use. Cuttings also give young plants of exactly the same character as the parent, whereas seed will give quite a variation of types, some of which may not be suitable for bonsai work.

In this book we are concerned only with stem cuttings (cuttings may also be made of leaves and roots) and these may be soft-wooded, half-ripe or hard-wooded. Half-ripe and hard-wooded are the types which are most frequently used for the propagation of the trees and shrubs chosen for bonsai work.

(i) *Half-ripe cuttings*. Small shoots of the current season's growth of about three to four inches long are torn off their 'parent' stem complete with a heel which is, in fact, part of the main or parent stem from which the shoot is growing. Half-ripe cuttings may also be made without a heel by cutting off the top three or four inches of the shoot just below a leaf joint or node, provided that the shoot at this point has begun to get firm but not woody. The bark should have become tough and darker in colour than at the growing tip. The lower leaves are removed before insertion to prevent them from decaying, and thus possibly damaging the stem (Fig. 10). All cuts, when trimming the heels of cutting and removing leaves, should be made carefully with a *very* sharp knife or razor blade. Rough

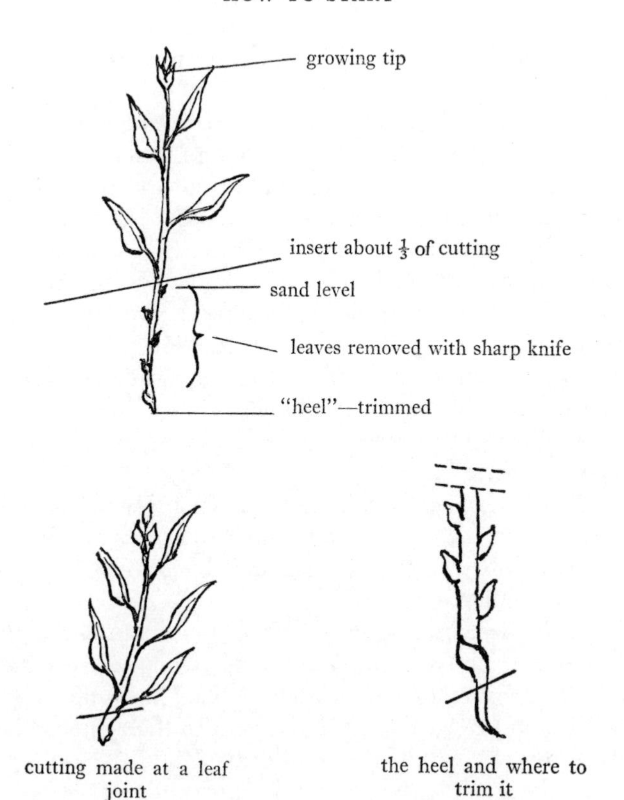

10. The making of semi-ripe cuttings

cuts and damaged tissues may cause the cutting to decay before rooting can start.

When only a few cuttings of each kind are taken, these are best inserted in a five-inch pot which has been given a generous layer of 'crocks' (see page 39) and then filled with sand or vermiculite which retains moisture well. Large quantities can be inserted in rows in boxes (kipper or sultana boxes are most suitable) prepared in the same way as the five-inch pots.

Each cutting is inserted firmly, approximately one-third of its length being buried. After insertion a thorough watering is given. The pots are placed in a cold frame and kept shaded in hot sun until rooting starts. The boxes should be covered with a sheet of glass, and newspaper if sunny. In this case the tops of the cuttings will need to be approximately one inch below the rim of the box. When rooting has taken place the glass may be removed gradually to increase ventilation.

When the cuttings are well rooted they must be potted. On no account should they be left too long in the rooting medium or they will begin to suffer from starvation, as sand contains no plant foods.

(ii) *Hard-wood cuttings.* This type of cutting is made when the season's growth has finished and the shoots are firm right to the tip. With deciduous subjects it is usual to wait till the leaves have fallen.

As a rule these cuttings are made from nine to twelve inches long and they must be fully ripe and strong as they have to stand the rigours of the winter. A heel may be kept and trimmed and the cutting should be cut to the required length at the top immediately above a dormant bud. These cuttings may also be made without a heel by trimming the shoot just below a bud. If the upper part of a shoot is used, it is advisable to remove the tip in order to encourage stronger growth in the spring following the insertion of the cutting. The ground should be forked carefully and then a narrow slit or gully is cut with a spade to a depth of five to six inches. A layer of coarse sand one inch deep scattered in the bottom of the gully will help root growth, especially in the heavier soils. Each cutting is pushed into the soil in the gully, buried to between half and two-thirds of its length. The soil should then be levelled and thoroughly firmed with the heel of the shoe or boot at the

Fagus crenata (Beech) grown as an Upright specimen. The small fern adds an interesting note to the base of the trunk; anything larger would have a detracting effect

time of planting, and again in the spring, as frosts will have loosened it during the winter. They often remain dormant, forming only a callus, until spring when roots will form and signs of growth can be seen in the leaves. Plants raised from hard-wood cuttings remain *in situ* until the following autumn —October or November—when they are potted.

As far as conifers are concerned, these are not always easily raised from cuttings. The high resin content of *Pinus*, *Picea* and *Abies* seems to hinder the formation of the callus from which the new roots grow, so these are more easily grown from seed. *Cupressus* and *Juniperus* on the other hand are not so resinous and the best results are obtained from semi-ripe cuttings taken in June or July; half of each cutting should be ripe. These cuttings may well need to stay in the rooting pots until the following spring before being potted.

Quicker and better root formation can in many cases be brought about by the use of rooting hormones. These hormones are made in various strengths, which should be related to the type or condition of the cuttings being made. One of the easiest to use and the best-tried is 'Seradix' B powder, which is available in three strengths—pink for soft cuttings, white for half-ripe cuttings, and grey for hard-wood cuttings. A very complete list of plants suitable for each strength is supplied with each tin of powder and the simple directions should, of course, be followed carefully.

Holly may be male, female or bisexual (having both male and female flowers on the same plant) and, of course, for bonsai work the bisexual is the type required if the bonsai is wanted for its berries as well as attractive foliage. In the case of male and female plants, the berries will not form unless the female flowers are cross-pollinated by the pollen from male flowers; this could naturally be a big difficulty for a town- or flat-dweller. It is for this reason that the *Ilex aquifolium* appears in the list below, for if a holly tree is known to be bisexual, identical plants may be produced by cuttings. Some forms of *I. aquifolium* are bisexual and it is from these that cuttings should be taken.

Chaenomeles is included in the list for both cuttings and layering, and indeed nurserymen usually keep what are known as 'stool' plants and the young shoots produced each year are layered. It is, however, possible to raise plants from hard-wood cuttings, though the percentage of success is less; in this particular case cuttings with a heel are usually more successful.

The following subjects are often raised from cuttings ('s' denotes semi-ripe and 'h' hard-wood cuttings):

DECIDUOUS	EVERGREEN
× *Chaenomeles* h	*Juniperus* s
× *Cotoneaster* h	*Cryptomeria* s
× *Forsythia* s and h	*Ilex aquifolium* s and h
× *Prunus subhirtella* s	
× *Salix* h	
Tamarix h	

4. LAYERING

Some plants whose shoots can be brought down to the soil may be increased quite easily by this method. A healthy shoot is selected, usually one a year old gives the best results, and a slit is cut in it about one inch long from parent plant to tip at a place where the shoot will touch the ground. It is then pegged down in such a way that the slit is kept open and the shoot firm. Finally the slit portion and peg are covered with two to three inches of good sandy soil which is firmed and watered (Fig. 11). A stake is sometimes necessary to keep the shoot firm, thereby avoiding damage to any young roots as they form.

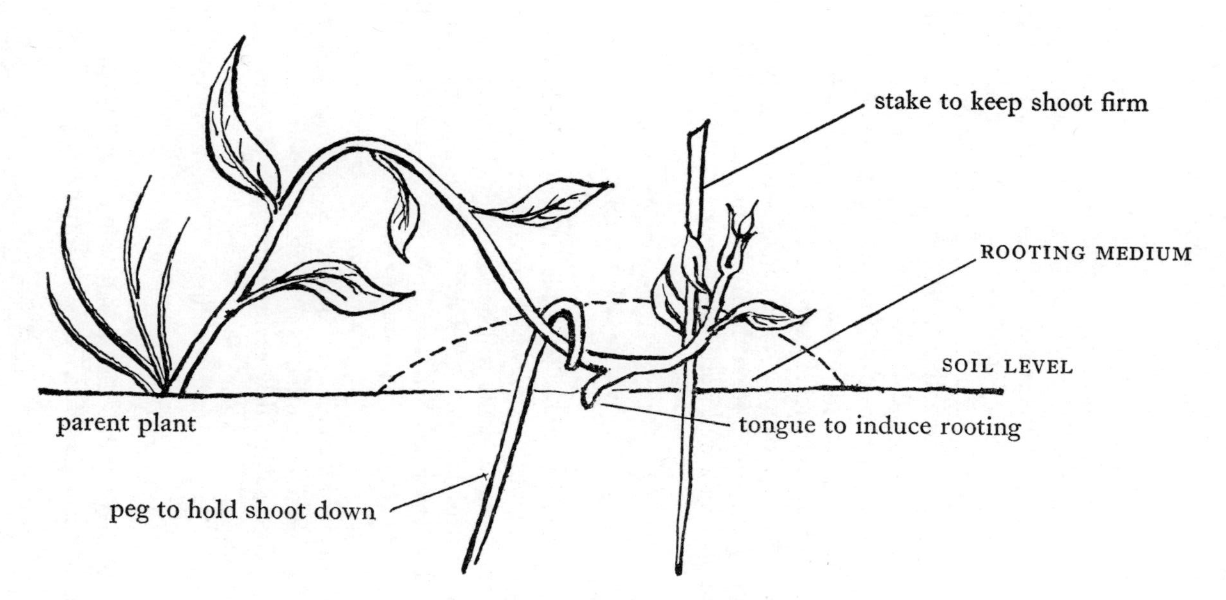

11. Method of layering

Spring, when growth has started, is the best time to layer and most plants will have formed good roots by the autumn. Two or three weeks before removing the new plant for potting, the shoot should be cut on the parent side of the split.

Azaleas, *Chaenomeles*, *Jasminum nudiflorum* and lilac are all quite readily reproduced by layering. Sometimes old plants of *Prunus amygdalus* (almond) and *P. persica* (peach) are found on their own roots, and these roots often send up suckers which can be dug up to form new plants. Nowadays selected varieties of both these prunus are usually on plum stocks, in which case the plum suckers are not of interest to the bonsai grower. However, people have sometimes been successful with sowing the stones from the fresh fruit, and suckers from any such plants are well worth digging up.

5. WILD PLANTS

The Japanese bonsai enthusiast is always on the lookout for plants growing in the wild which could be potted and grown on as bonsai; these plants will be seedlings of trees or shrubs rather than wild flowers. Occasionally in this country also one may find a specimen with an interesting shape—gnarled, twisted or windswept; but owing to the fact that these plants are usually not young, they are not easy to transplant and re-establish in containers. Their roots have often penetrated the soil to considerable depths, even if the soil is poor, and one cannot avoid causing fairly severe damage to the plants when lifting them.

It is quite easy to find seedlings of a number of British trees, particularly sycamore, hawthorn, holly, silver birch, beech and various willows. *Salix lapponum* (Downy Willow) and *S. myrsinites* (Whortle Leaved Willow) can be found on the fells of the Lake District and Scottish moors. Naturally

A Cascading *Juniperus prostrata glauca.* Several strands of thinner wire have been used in place of one thick wire. In the course of time a more attractive curve should be formed. More shoots could be thinned out with advantage

the smaller the plant in question the greater the chance of success in re-establishing it in its new environment.

When digging up a wild plant do it, if possible, before growth starts in the spring, and retain as much soil as possible in a 'ball' round the roots by enclosing them in a piece of sacking or polythene (see page 41). Readers may, of course, find good wild specimens when they are out walking or on holiday at any time of the year, and if this happens they will often find it is possible to re-establish a plant even if it is in full leaf. A little extra after-care will be necessary; if possible soak the ground well before digging up the plant and water the soil when it has been planted or potted. It will be worth keeping the plant shaded from the sun and syringing it copiously two or three times a day to cut down the loss of moisture from the leaves which if excessive will cause wilting. The next stage is to plant the selected tree in the open ground in good soil that has had peat or other humus added to encourage the development of a new and fibrous root system. After a year in this site, and if the plant has recovered from the disturbance, it may be transferred to a suitable container. If the wild tree selected is a relatively small specimen with a fibrous root system, it will be possible to plant it into a pot rather than in open soil. It is advisable to use an ordinary flower pot rather than the eventual bonsai container; the greater soil capacity will facilitate quicker recovery. After a growing season the plant will have recovered from the disturbance and grown new fibrous roots.

Bonsai grown from selected 'old' wild plants will need very little training; just enough to maintain the shape. As far as the younger specimens are concerned, all training should be delayed for a year. If wire is applied too soon, it may cause branches to die or even cause the death of the plant.

Now that the main ways of starting a bonsai specimen have been discussed, the reader will realize that care, patience and time are needed for the start of a successful specimen. As mentioned at the beginning of this chapter, it is now possible to buy bonsai that have had the initial training done. This of course saves time and trouble, but at the same time removes one of the chief delights of bonsai growing. Naturally a bonsai that one has raised and trained right from the beginning is going to give the greatest pleasure and satisfaction.

4
Containers, Soil, Potting and Repotting

The choice of container will be very largely a matter of personal taste. There are, however, a few points which must be taken into consideration when trying to select the most suitable container, and we should not lose sight of the meaning of the word bonsai; 'bon' means shallow pan, and so it is important to keep the pot as shallow as possible; too deep a container will look especially ugly when planted with a small bonsai.

Shape. The top surface area of soil should be kept in proportion to the size of the plant. For single upright specimens a round or oval container is suitable; but where more than one tree is grown in a container, or when the oblique or cascade style is chosen, a rectangular shape is usually more artistic and pleasing to look at. The size and shape of containers chosen are dependent on the question of proportion, and the grower should let this be his guide. Some pot-making firms still produce oval, square and oblong seed and alpine pans and these can also be found sometimes second-hand in sales. (Fig. 12)

Glazing. Glazing is a matter of great importance. In almost all cases bonsai will thrive best and longest in completely unglazed containers. In Japan there are potteries that design and make bonsai containers and these are always unglazed inside. With the growing interest in bonsai in this country it may well

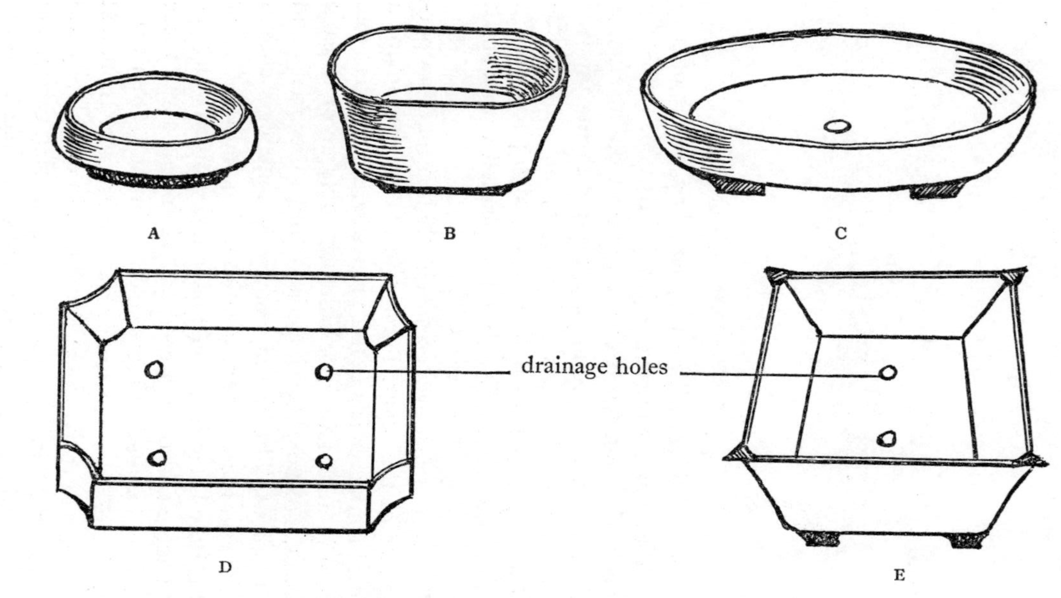

12. Containers vary in size and shape and should be selected to suit each individual bonsai

Oblique *Cedrus atlantica glauca*

happen that more potteries here will again make unglazed containers especially for bonsai; they are also most suitable for bulbs.

Drainage. It is most important to have a drainage hole in each container. A small pot will only need one hole, but a larger one may well need more. Holes can be made by very carefully drilling with a hand-drill and this will often be necessary if containers are bought in antique or bric-a-bric shops. It is always worth looking in these places for suitable containers as often a 'pot' may be found to suit a particular specimen.

Colour. The colour of the container can do much to enhance the appearance of the specimen, but it should always be as natural as possible—i.e. shades of black, brown and green; in a few cases white can be most effective. On the whole evergreen specimens look their best when *not* seen in a green container. When a container is to be chosen for a flowering bonsai, the colour of the flowers must naturally be considered. For example, if a pink or red *Chaenomeles* is to be potted, containers of the common earthenware flower-pot colour need to be avoided, and a forsythia would not look well in a container of a yellowish shade.

Ornaments. These can so much more easily detract from the appearance of the bonsai than add to it, that they should be avoided. The Japanese seldom use them and when they do the ornaments selected are very small and usually of antique origin.

Soils. Most bonsai will remain in the same pots undisturbed for a year; some for two or three years. During this time they will be watered and fed frequently. For this reason it is important that the compost used should be of such a form that it does not become waterlogged or sour. The John Innes Potting Compost No. 1 is a good safe standard compost to use; but if readers feel that they would like to make up one of their own, the following proportions will give a good mixture:

2 parts good, fresh fibrous loam.
2 parts *coarse* river sand.
1 part leaf mould.

The soil eventually used should not pack down too hard in the pan as this excludes air which is vital for the healthy growth of the tree.

Potting. As a general guide it is safe to say that bonsai are best potted or repotted while they are dormant—just before growth starts in the spring.

Before potting up a seedling or repotting an older specimen, water it thoroughly an hour or so beforehand. The compost to be used should be moist enough to bind when squeezed in the hand, but not so wet that it will not crumble again easily between the fingers. The drainage holes should be covered with broken clay pots (curved side uppermost) or zinc gauze disks, and these in turn covered with root fibre to prevent the soil washing into the drainage holes.

The container may be considered in the same light as a picture-frame and, having discussed the shape and colour of this 'frame', we can now look at the position of the subject in it. The perfectly shaped, upright bonsai is best planted in the centre and when one is potting all bonsai, care should be taken to see that the best side of the tree is kept to the front. Bonsai of the Cascading style need planting to one side—that over which they cascade. (Fig. 13) If a tree is more heavily branched on one side, it is best planted off centre so that the heavier side is over the largest proportion of soil.

As far as group planting is concerned, the highest plant should be about one-third of the way in from the edge of the container. (Fig. 14)

When potting, make the compost fall evenly among the roots by sharply tapping the 'pot' on the bench and then firming with the fingers, leaving about a third of an inch space for watering; in some cases a small pointed (not too sharp)

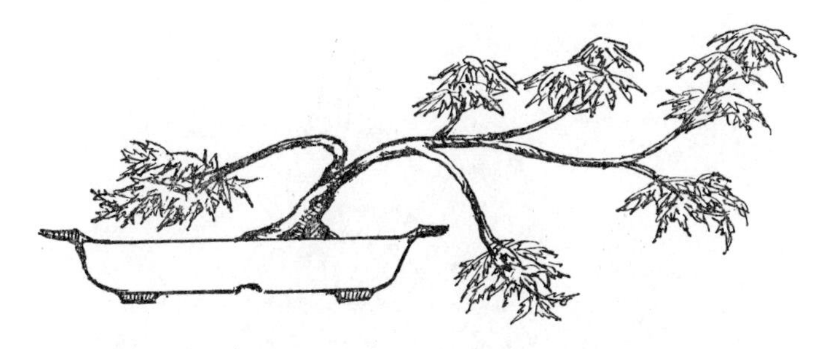

13. Cascading bonsai planted off-centre

stick will help get the soil into all the crevices; the Japanese use chopsticks.

If suitable attractive chippings or pebbles can be found to spread on the soil surface, these will often help to prevent it becoming hard or 'panned' with frequent watering. Sometimes a few very carefully selected pebbles or miniature rocks to one side or end of the container look more attractive, though of course these do not fulfil quite the same function.

After potting, water thoroughly and keep evenly moist thereafter. If the plant is an evergreen, or a deciduous plant with leaves, keep it shaded from hot sun until it is well established. In very hot and dry spells frequent syringing with a fine mist will be very beneficial.

Repotting. The soil, method of potting and after-care are the same for repotting as for potting, but one or two things need to be considered.

Repotting bonsai does not necessarily mean transferring to a larger container, as this may promote too much growth. For bonsai which are not in the very early stages of training the same container may be used with partly new soil. If the specimen is in need of rejuvenating, it is advisable to remove all old soil from the roots and replace it with fresh compost. Fast-

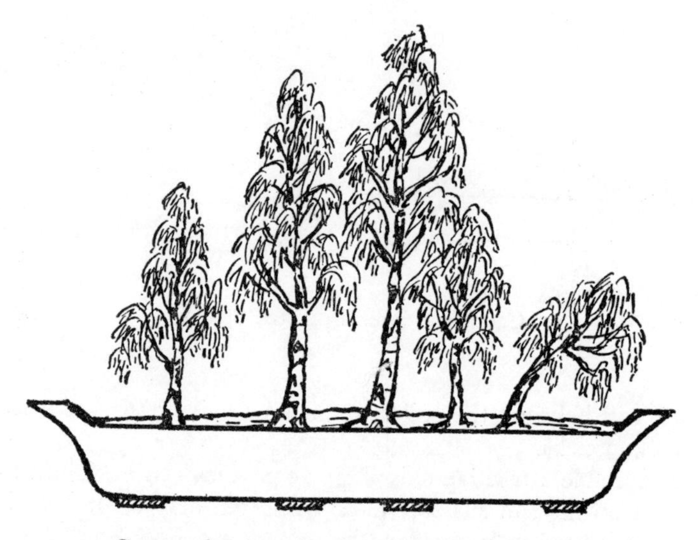

14. Group planting showing position of tallest plant (see pp. 54 and 89)

growing plants, including most deciduous trees and shrubs, need repotting every year; slower-growing plants, including most conifers, may need repotting only every two to three years. Bonsai that are pot-bound, or those that give indications that the soil is sour or too hard packed and airless, must be repotted as soon as these points are noticed, but the best time to do this work is undoubtedly just before the season's growth starts.

When repotting is to be done, the plant should be watered a few hours beforehand so that the soil has drained before the removal of the container. This is done by holding the stem between the fingers of the left hand and then turning the container upside down and giving it a sharp tap on the potting-bench or table.

First of all remove all old drainage material and then about one-third of the old soil, mostly from the bottom, but also a little of the original surface soil. It may be necessary to use a pointed stick, similar to a chopstick, to remove the soil from between some of the roots. Any long roots exposed should next be trimmed with a sharp knife or secateurs, to leave about a one-inch space between them and the side of the container, which will be filled with the fresh compost.

The actual method of repotting is as for potting, and similar drainage must be provided. It is most important to repot the specimen at the same depth as before. After repotting, water the plant and keep it in a cool shady place, taking care not to overwater it as the roots will not be very active until they have re-established themselves; syringing in hot weather will help the plant to recover from the disturbance. Any necessary pruning or wiring is best postponed until the following year so that the plant suffers no further set-backs, unless it starts into very vigorous growth during the summer.

5
Training

Material and tools required:

Raffia

String

Copper wire. Various thicknesses are available and for young trunks and branches gauge 18, 19 or 20 is usually adequate; for older, thicker trunks something heavier will be needed. It is a help to remember that the lower the gauge number the thicker the wire; in fact, the numbers used correspond to those used for knitting-needles. Copper wire is the best type as it does not rust or damage the bark, unless it is left on too long, in which case it will gradually cut into it. It soon loses the characteristic lustre and tones in with the tree. Plastic-coated wire can be obtained, but there is not usually such a varied range of thicknesses and the plastic itself never seems to tone in so well as the uncovered wire. Copper wire may be obtained at most wireless and electrical shops. The author finds the cable used for wiring a house for electricity most useful, because this is made of a number of wires of varying thicknesses. The plastic insulation used to contain them is easily removed with a sharp knife.

Wire cutters

Scissors—sharp and pointed

Sharp knife

Secateurs

Split bamboo canes

In most cases training may start as soon as it is possible to fix the wire or tie the stem to a cane. It is much easier to start with a soft pliable young plant than an old one with bark and stem that have become hard and brittle; but some trees, e.g. willow, have very soft bark and may be damaged if wired too young.

Treatment of copper wire. Before using copper wire one should burn it in a low heat to make it more pliable and thus easier to twist round the branches. Where only a gas ring is available the wire can be left on this if it is turned to its lowest, and in an all-electric house similarly the wire can be placed on a ring set at the lowest heat. The wire will gradually change colour and will bend quite easily after a few minutes' heating. Remember that it will be very hot; so do not pick it up with bare fingers until it has cooled.

Some specimens will have bark that damages rather easily and in these cases the wire should be wrapped round with strips of paper to give added protection. This, of course, will have to be done after the wire has been heated.

Once in place, it gradually regains its original strength and rigidity. If the wire is ever to be reused, it will need to be heated again. When the time for removing the wire comes, great care will have to be taken, as branches can so easily be snapped because the wire will have regained its original stiffness.

Bonsai are created by a combination of training by wiring and tying, and dwarfing by pruning; both processes will need to be carried out simultaneously, but it will be easier to treat them separately in this book.

The best time to start training deciduous trees is during the growing season when the leaves are fully grown. If shoots need wiring to bring them into the desired position and shape, they should be at least two inches long; anything shorter may easily be damaged during the wiring process. Evergreens are, however, best wired in the autumn or winter.

When one is wiring trunks or branches, a wire no thicker than is necessary to keep them in place should be used. If a branch is to be wired, wind the wire round the trunk several times to fix it and then round the branch. Do not wind too close to the growing point as this can easily be damaged, but extend the wire beyond the tip by about half an inch so that the winding can be continued as the shoot grows. To avoid splitting at the point where the branch grows from the trunk, hold this place very firmly with one hand while winding with the other. The coils should be evenly spaced about a quarter of an inch apart and firm, but not marking the bark. (Fig. 15) The wire will be needed for several years and rewinding may well be necessary after as little as six months to avoid damaging and marking the bark. Slow-growing trees may be left with the

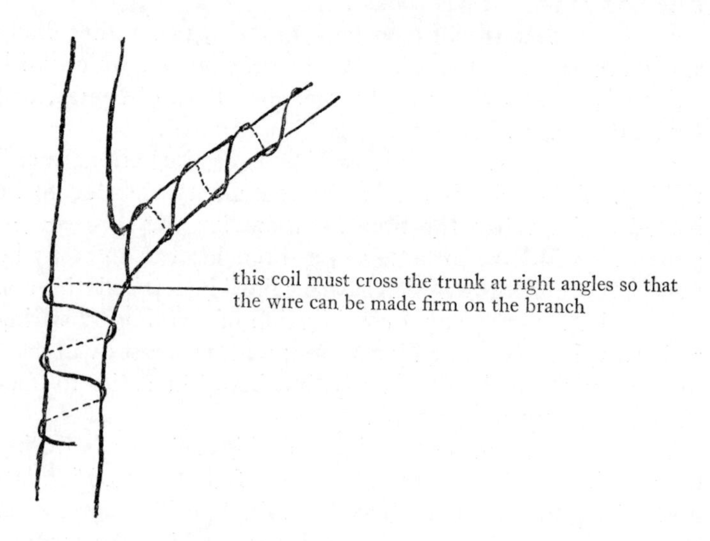

15. Method of wiring a branch. Note the even spacing of the wire

Chamaecyparis pisifera squarrosa in the 'Broom' form of the Upright style. Shoot-pinching has formed plenty of attractive young glaucous-blue foliage

same wire for as much as a year. Before rewinding let a few months pass so that the bark may grow unhindered and recover from any possible marking.

TRAINING OF THE VARIOUS STYLES

When deciding on the shape for a specimen, it is always more satisfactory to choose one that is in character with the species in question; for example, do not try to make an Upright bonsai of a weeping willow or a Cascading one of a beech or sycamore.

UPRIGHT AND OBLIQUE STYLES

In the case of both these styles little or no wiring will be needed to shape the trunk; this can be done by tying it with raffia to a cane in the upright position. These ties should be remade from time to time to prevent damage to the plant by constriction as the stem swells. The branches may need a little wiring to guide them into the desired position, but it will not need to be left on very long.

THE CASCADING STYLE

When the stem of a Cascading bonsai is being trained, a stout wire should be pushed into the soil to the base of the container and then bent over the side at the desired angle. The trunk is then gradually persuaded into this shape by frequent ties made along its length: these can be tightened gradually throughout the season. The ties will exert considerable pressure on the bark and should therefore have a protective pad of rubber placed under them. Strong raffia or string may be used. The branches will need wiring carefully into attractive

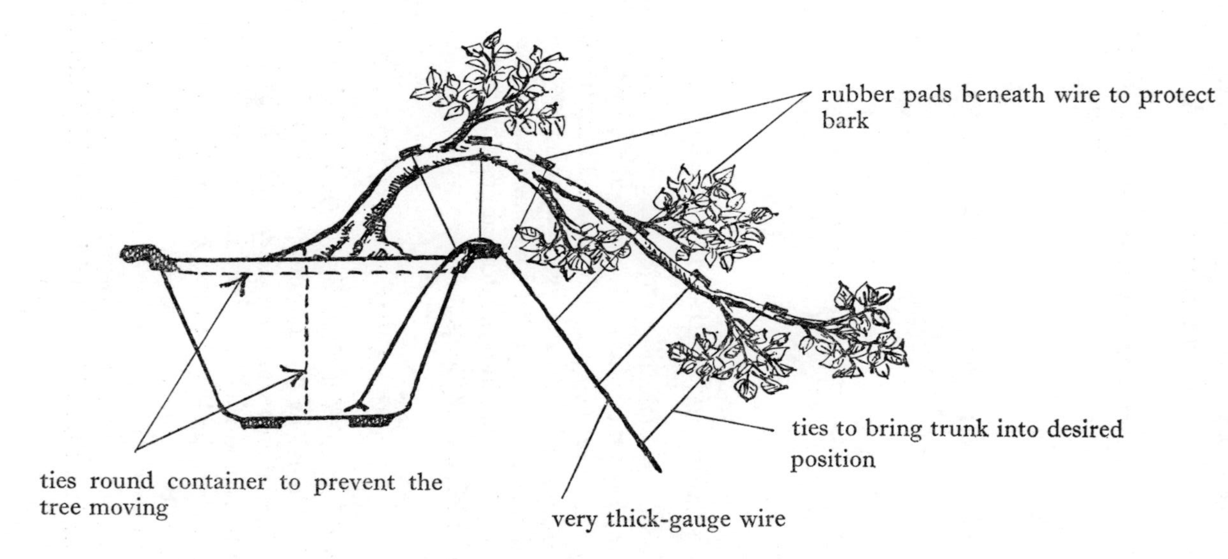

16. The training of a Cascading bonsai

positions as their original ones may look strange when the trunk reaches its own new position (Fig. 16).

THE WINDING TRUNK STYLE

The Winding trunk bonsai is formed by winding wire round the stem and bending it gradually first to one side and then to the other (never backwards and forwards). (Fig. 17)

The Japanese often start with a plant four to five years old, but most people attempting the style for the first time will find it easier to form if they start training the tree when it is two, three or four years old, before the trunk becomes too thick.

THE GNARLED TRUNK STYLE

The most complicated style to train is the Gnarled (Hankan). This is not only winding but also gnarled and twisted; for this reason it takes very much longer to create. Both wire and cane will be needed, and a reasonably pliable trunk.

If possible the lower part of the trunk should be brought down to the soil level and then twisted round the canes. These twists will *in time* give the gnarled appearance. The canes should be pushed well into the container to keep them firm. If an older tree is being trained, it will be easier to do it while it is still growing in the garden, as the canes can be kept really firm in the deep soil. The ties will need remaking and tightening several times a year for two or three years. (Fig. 18)

In both the Winding and Gnarled styles the branches will need training with wire to make them fit in attractively. Some branches will have to be removed entirely, as if too many are left the resulting effect will be crowded and confused.

17. Showing the side to side bends of the trunk of a Winding bonsai (see p. 63)

THE CLASPED-TO-STONE STYLE

When attempting to form a Clasped-to-Stone bonsai, a young plant with active and preferably long roots will give the best hope for success. The most suitable kind of stone is a fairly soft one with crevices and grooves in which the roots can settle. It should be pleasing in shape and if possible larger at the base than at the top; this will make it easier to fix firmly in the soil. The container should be a shallow one, but its shape will depend very largely on the shape and size of the stone selected and the tree to be grown. The bonsai grower should always try to have an image in his mind of the final product he is aiming to create.

Chamaecyparis pisifera plumosa. A 25-year-old plant forming a dense umbrella-shaped top

Spring, soon after the growth starts, is the safest time to fix the roots to the stone. Conifers may, if necessary, be fixed in the autumn. In all cases the trees must be well watered before being disturbed. First of all the surface of the stone should be smeared with a clay or soil paste, filling all the little crevices and holes. Next the soil is shaken off the tree roots. The

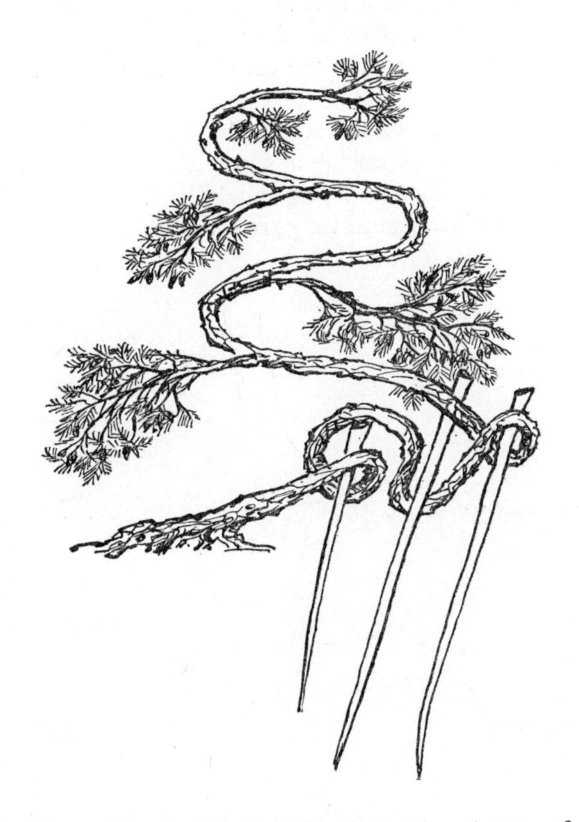

18. The training of a Gnarled bonsai showing the use of pegs. The ties have been omitted for clarity's sake (see p. 63)

longest roots are taken down any grooves or crevices; the very longest ones may be fixed under the stone. (Fig. 19) A soft garden twine can be used to keep the roots in place, and then another layer of soil 'paste' is painted over them. Finally moss, preferably sphagnum or something similar, is packed over the roots until the tree is settled; it is best to remove the moss as soon as the tree is settled, because if it is left the roots will grow into it. As time passes the roots will take the shape of the stone and grow down into the soil in the container and all ties may be removed.

After being fixed to the stone, the tree will benefit from frequent syringing, especially in sunny weather. To start with the soil will not need watering much, as the roots will only take up water slowly until they are settled.

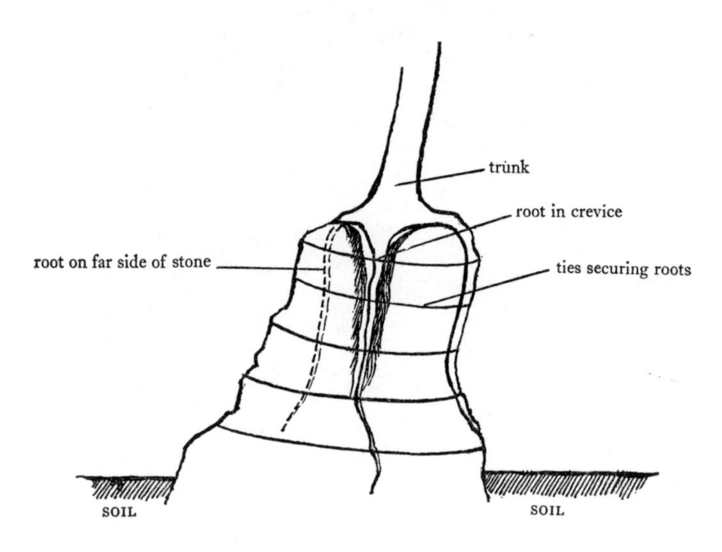

19. Fixing the roots to the stone of a Clasped-to-Stone bonsai

Once the tree is settled on the stone, training the trunk may continue in the normal way for whatever style has been chosen. The Japanese maples have given some very good results in this style.

IKADI–BUKI STYLE

This is quite an easy style to attempt and little or no wiring will be needed. Deciduous or coniferous trees may be used and there are two ways of starting an Ikadi–buki bonsai. The first

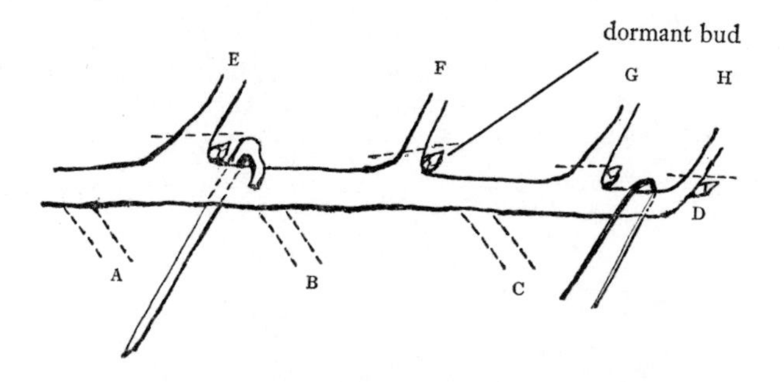

20. A trunk laid horizontally and being prepared for the Ikadi-buki style (see p. 68)
A, B, C, D=removed branches
E, F, G, H=may be removed when buds grow out

is to choose a dormant tree with plenty of buds and plant it so that the main trunk and the lowest branches are lying on the soil surface and partly buried. The lower branches are removed entirely and so also is the leading shoot. The upper branches may be removed if desired, leaving dormant buds in the angle between branch and trunk to grow out and form the 'forest'. Alternatively the upper branches may be left and trained by wiring and pruning to form the 'forest'. The trunk and pruned branches can be kept down in the soil by placing ties over them and round the container in several places. Care should be taken not to damage the bark; a piece of rubber or similar material can be placed between the bark and the tie. Wire 'hairpins' may also be used. This method is best suited to deciduous trees.

The second method, suitable for conifers, is to choose a well-branched tree and plant it on its side in the container, having first removed the branches that would be on the under side of the horizontal trunk. These branches should be cut off cleanly close to the trunk, which should then be buried to half its width (Fig. 20). The remaining branches on the upper side will then need the usual training. Sometimes, if the branches are too close, it will be necessary to thin some out.

Whichever method is used, the tree should be kept shaded and syringed in hot sunny weather until it is really settled.

Chamaecyparis obtusa. Good use has been made of moss and stones with this tree

6
Dwarfing

The wiring that has just been described is primarily intended to train the tree into the desired shape, but it does also have a *slight* dwarfing effect. This is because a branch which is bent out of its natural line has its flow of sap checked, and this in turn slows the rate of growth according to the severity of the bending. It is on the various forms of pruning that bonsai mainly depend for their dwarfing; i.e. shoot-pinching, leaf-pinching, root-pruning and pruning during dormancy. Conifers should not be pruned too severely when they are fully grown, but deciduous trees and shrubs will stand quite hard pruning and produce replacement shoots. When one is pruning, the cut is made just above a node (leaf joint), care being taken not to damage the bud which lies between the shoot and the leaf axil (Fig. 21). Equal care must be taken when pinching out shoots during the growing season.

It is most important to remember that a bonsai should not be starved to keep it small, but kept active by careful feeding and watering (see Chapter 7). A starved plant will be a sickly, and therefore unhealthy, plant.

Another point to remember here is that, although the size of a plant can be controlled by various forms of pruning, the size of the flowers and fruit will remain almost unchanged; the quinces and crab apples will look large sometimes when compared with the size of the plant. This can, however, be a rather interesting 'discrepancy'.

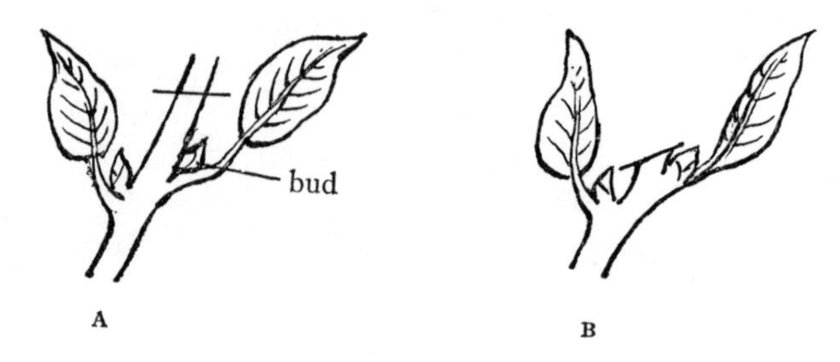

21. Methods of pruning. Incorrect (A) and correct (B) (see p. 69)

SHOOT-PINCHING

This pinching is started in the spring when the young shoots are about an inch long, and helps to balance the shape of the tree. By removing part of the shoots leaves are also removed, and it is this that helps to dwarf the tree, as the leaves manufacture food from nutrients and water taken up from the soil by the roots. The very tip of the shoot is removed with the fingers, nails, or sharp, pointed scissors, taking care not to crush the remaining stem; in the case of conifers with needles, do not

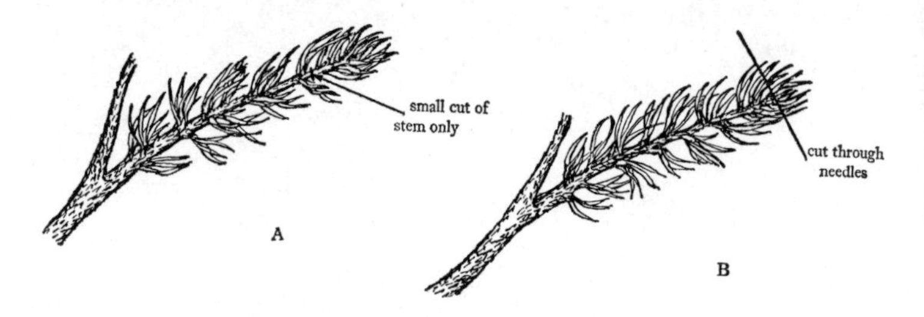

22. Shoot-pinching of conifers
Correct (A) and incorrect (B)

cut through the needles as this can be most ugly. (Fig. 22)

The tree, if active and healthy, will send out more shoots which in turn may be pinched or removed entirely. The latter may well be necessary in many cases to prevent overcrowding. This secondary growth also very often produces smaller leaves

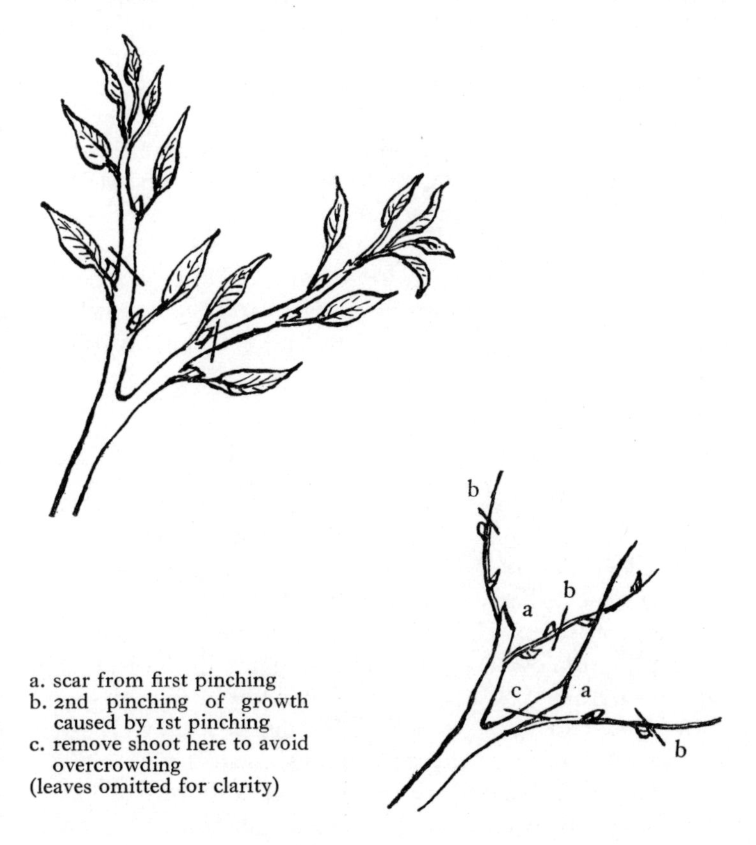

23. Shoot-pinching of deciduous subjects.

than the first early growth, and these will be more in proportion to the size of the tree; it is most effective with trees such as beech, maples, oaks and other deciduous trees. Some very vigorous trees will keep producing shoots and these must be pinched as soon as they are an inch long. Do not allow them to grow any longer, because the resulting scar will take longer to heal over. (Fig. 23)

Naturally the shoots will not all grow at exactly the same rate, so pinching cannot all be done at the same time, but must be spread over a period, pinching each shoot when it is about an inch long. Weak trees should not be pinched too hard and should receive a little extra attention with careful manuring to strengthen them.

When pinching flowering trees and shrubs, remember to pinch early as the resulting growths will carry the flower buds for the next season; e.g. forsythia, apricot, peach, *Chaenomeles*, etc.

LEAF-PINCHING

This additional method of inducing dense dwarf growth is only used on the most vigorous deciduous trees; maples respond to it particularly well. If the tree is really strong, all the leaves may be removed, leaving a quarter inch of the leaf stalk which will wither and fall off, and the buds in the leaf axils will grow out. In this way a false dormant or leafless season is created and two years' growth is produced in one. If such drastic treatment is considered too harsh, half the leaves may be removed either by actually halving each leaf or by pinching off alternate leaves. Leaf-pinching is only done once in any one growing season and when the tree is in its most active state—mid June to July usually—and when the base of the shoots have begun to harden. After leaf-pinching the bonsai needs to be protected from excessive rain, but exposed to the sun; too much rain may cause the soil to become stale and airless, as no water is being given off through the leaves. When the new growth appears feeding may start again and shoot-pinching must be carried out for the rest of the season as and when necessary. The new leaves will be smaller and more proportionate to the size of the bonsai.

ROOT-PRUNING

It is through the roots that a plant gets both water and plant food in solution. The larger the tree the larger the root system it has; hence it follows that if the root system is reduced, the size of the tree may be kept in check because the food and water supply is reduced. When a tree is allowed to grow naturally, the root system will usually spread out to approximately the same distance as the branches, hence it would seem reasonable to keep the root system of a bonsai well pruned to correspond to the desired 'spread' of the top growth.

When a wild plant or nursery plant is dug up, a certain amount of root-pruning is automatically carried out and this is one reason why a newly lifted plant is checked. Bonsai growers, however, do some intentional pruning whenever they repot a specimen. The roots are trimmed to leave a space of about an inch between them and the side of the pot or container. This has been described in Chapter 4 on page 57. The vigorous trees are repotted more frequently and so undergo more root-pruning.

PRUNING DURING DORMANCY

If pinching during the growing season has been carefully carried out, very little winter pruning will be necessary. Very weak, dead, unwanted or ugly shoots are removed, but severe pruning should be avoided as it promotes strong, sappy growth which is undesirable in bonsai work.

Only the most essential winter pruning should be done on spring-flowering shrubs, as flower buds are bound to be reduced. When possible these plants should be pruned *after* flowering. Peaches, apricots and cherries sometimes die as a result of winter pruning; so any necessary cutting on this group is best done in the summer.

When one is removing any branch with knife or secateurs, it is most important to make a good 'clean' cut, leaving no 'snag' which not only looks unsightly, but may decay and possibly damage the trunk.

7
Watering and Manuring

WATERING

The watering of any potted plant has always been rather a stumbling block, but with time and experience it really does become easier. It is not possible to set down any hard-and-fast rules, because the frequency of watering depends on so many things, and so the subject is mainly a matter of common sense.

A small can with a narrow spout and a fine rose will be needed and rain-water is the best water to use, if it is obtainable, as it suits all plants. Should it not be available, tap water must be used, but if it contains lime azaleas should not be grown as they are lime haters.

How often a bonsai needs water depends on the soil mixture and drainage; it has been emphasized earlier that drainage must be very carefully arranged and the mixture needs to be what is called 'open', that is, rather coarse, containing a coarse gritty sand. If it is too fine, it will become hard and stale with frequent watering and then the roots will not make adequate healthy growth. Very small containers dry out much more quickly than larger ones, and whether they are glazed or unglazed will also affect the speed of drying out.

The daily weather also has a great effect on watering and so has the type of plant being grown. Broad-leaved, deciduous trees use more water than trees with narrow, needle-like leaves, e.g. pines. The following list gives only an approximate guide to the water requirements of a bonsai throughout the year:

Winter—once a week.
Spring—once a day.
Early summer—twice a day.
Mid-summer—three times a day.
Late summer—once or twice a day.
Autumn—once or twice a week.

One question that is always being asked is, 'What is the best way to water a plant in a pot? The answer is to water the soil surface from the top. The space between the soil and the top of the container is filled up, if necessary several times, until the water comes out of the drainage holes at the bottom of the container; this method ensures that the entire soil mixture is evenly and adequately watered.

Some people may find it difficult to decide when a bonsai needs watering, and it is hard to make any definite suggestions. As a rule when the soil looks dry and is just coming *very slightly* away from the edge of the container the plant needs watering. Sometimes, however, with certain soils the compost will appear light in colour and dry on the surface, but may not need watering. The author usually taps each container gently with a small wooden hammer or flicks the rim with a fingernail. If the resulting noise has a ringing tone to it, then water is needed; if, on the other hand, the noise is a 'dead' thud, water should be withheld for a while.

Overwatering is a risk and can be as disastrous as lack of water, since the soil is apt to become airless and sour, and these conditions are not conducive to good root performance. If a plant is suffering from acute water shortage and is drooping, it should be put in the shade, syringed copiously two or three times a day and watered until the soil is evenly moist. The

A very much older plant of *Chamaecyparis obtusa* than shown in plate 11. A very well balanced specimen, the upper left balancing the lower right

syringing should be repeated for several days, especially in hot, dry weather.

If an attractive moss can be found to put on the soil surface, it will help to conserve moisture, but it should not detract in any way from the interest of the bonsai.

When summer holidays necessitate leaving the bonsai uncared for, the best solution is to plunge the container to the rim in a shady spot in the garden, but *not* one sheltered from the rain.

A small hand syringe capable of making a fine spray is a valuable piece of equipment for a bonsai enthusiast. In hot weather a thorough syringing early in the morning and in the evening will help keep the foliage fresh, but avoid syringing in the hot sun as this can lead to scorching, which appears as brown areas on the leaves. Some plants, however, should not be syringed too much since they may, as a result, produce too much sappy growth rather than flower buds, e.g. crab apples, quinces and *Chaenomeles*.

MANURING

The good growth of any plant depends on an adequate water supply and a balanced diet of plant foods, the most important of these being nitrogen, phosphate and potash. There are other foods needed by a plant, but they are nearly always available in suitable quantities in a good soil mixture.

Nowadays soluble or solid, organic or inorganic *complete* fertilizers are available in balanced forms from all horticultural sundriesmen. The soluble forms are quick-acting, whereas the solid forms applied to the surface of the soil are slower and more long lasting. The latter are not suitable if moss has been used on the soil surface, and they also tend to form a layer or crust, which will need breaking up with a blunt stick or label.

The proprietary brands of fertilizers will carry very careful instructions and these MUST be followed accurately. On the average the soluble forms may be applied once a week from spring to the end of summer. The solid forms, being slower and longer lasting, will only need applying once a month. In the case of very small containers the frequency of applications may be slightly increased on account of the very frequent watering that will be necessary; this watering is bound to 'leach' or wash out a certain amount of the fertilizer.

Japanese bonsai growers make up rather complicated organic manures from materials that are not readily available in this country, and so it is wiser to be content to obtain a good balanced mixture from sundriesmen.

Another warning must be given here: take care not to over-feed as this will lead to too much soft, sappy growth and in extreme cases to sickliness and even the death of the plant. If over-feeding is suspected, stop feeding, use plain water for several days running and give no more manure until the plant shows considerable signs of recovery.

Any fertilizers should be applied to the soil only, as leaves may easily be scorched, especially the young foliage; these scorched areas do not recover.

8
Some Typical Bonsai

In the following chapter a few easily obtainable trees and shrubs are taken individually and the methods of early training are described. Some of the subjects are not necessarily the best for forming a *perfect* bonsai (e.g. *Acer pseudoplatanus*), but are easily grown and will stand up to the first efforts of bonsai beginners. They also form quite pleasing specimens in as little as two or three years.

FLOWERING SHRUBS

CHAENOMELES LAGENARIA (FLOWERING QUINCE)

Style. Cascading and other informal styles. Flowers in March and April.

Potting. The young selected plant should be potted in March or September. A layered plant could be lifted in September or March, whereas rooted hardwood cuttings would be ready for lifting in the September after insertion. Seedlings are best potted in spring just before they start growth. (Fig. 24)

Wiring. This is most easily done in the growing season, May to June. If it is not done at this time for any reason, it can be done quite effectively at any time except during the winter.

Shoot-nipping and pruning. Any unnecessary shoots should be removed entirely in late June. If the nipping is done earlier,

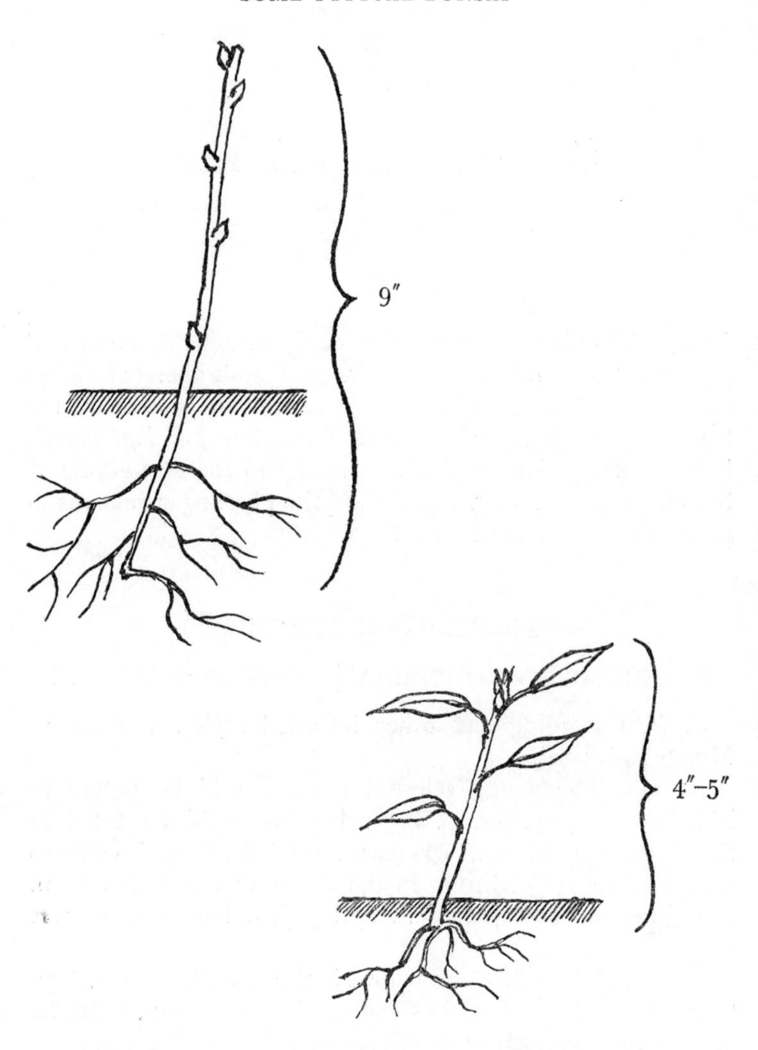

24. Rooted cutting of *Chaenomeles* or *Forsythia* in September, after insertion and in the following spring (see p. 82)

This *Pinus sylvestris* could be improved by some judicious shoot thinning

flower buds are not formed. When the shoots chosen to remain have six or seven leaf joints, these can be pruned at that point. Any resulting secondary growth must be pinched to one or two leaves or removed entirely. (Figs. 25, 26). When the flower buds are sufficiently formed it is sometimes necessary to thin them out so that the flowers are not spoilt by overcrowding.

Pinching in the second and following season is done at the second leaf always.

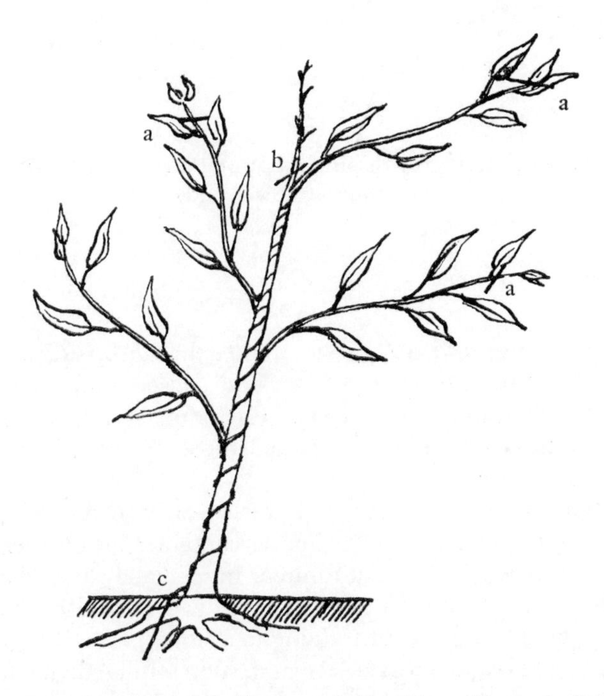

25. Initial pruning of *Chaenomeles* or *Forsythia* and similar subjects: (a) shoots pruned at 6th leaf, (b) growing tip removed as it starts to grow, (c) note that the wire has been pushed into the soil before winding (see p. 82)

Watering and feeding. Chaenomeles should be watered fairly freely, but not fed too much, as growth buds rather than flower buds will be formed by overfeeding. Plenty of sun helps the ripening of the wood and the formation of flower buds.

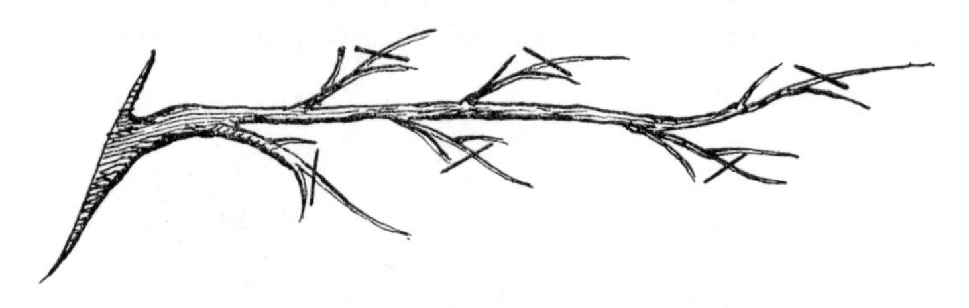

26. Secondary growth pinched at 2nd leaf to encourage formation of flower buds

FORSYTHIA SUSPENSA

Style. F. suspensa is suggested rather than *F. spectabile* as it has a less stiff and erect growth, and consequently it is admirably suited to the Oblique and Cascading styles. It is also a good species to train in the Clasped-to-Stone style. It flowers in March and April.

Potting. Because forsythias flower so early in the year, the best time to pot them in the bonsai container, or fix them on the stone, is either in the autumn or immediately after flowering, before the leaves get too well developed. (See also Chapter 5, page 64, for method of training to a stone.)

Wiring. This is most easily and successfully done in the growing season.

Shoot-nipping. Figs. 24, 25, 26. In the first growing season all selected shoots are cut at the sixth or seventh joint, when these are fully formed. After the flowers have fallen in subsequent years, any ugly or unwanted shoots must be removed and the flowering shoots be reduced to two leaves. Towards the end of the summer, when growth has stopped, any new shoots which will not be required for flowering the following spring must also be removed; the remainder are cut back, leaving one or two leaves. Pinching is not carried out during the growing period as it is at this time the flower buds form. The specimen may become rather shaggy looking, but as it will not be needed for display except when in flower this will not matter.

Sometimes after a number of years forsythias may be so full of flower buds that they produce very few shoots; if this should happen, it is an advantage to prune before flowering is over. In order to rejuvenate a *very* 'growth-shy' specimen it would be worth forgoing a season's flower by pruning hard early in the season *before* flowering.

When basal shoots appear on the main stem, these should be carefully retained and used to replace older and possibly weak shoots.

After five or six years, and more, the specimen need only be about twelve inches high, because shoots have been cut to two leaves, removed entirely, or cut back into older wood to rejuvenate branches when necessary.

JASMINUM NUDIFLORUM (WINTER JASMINE, FLOWERS IN JANUARY AND FEBRUARY)

Style. Winter jasmine is suitable for most styles, but in Japan it is very much favoured for the Clasped-to-Stone style and indeed the roots are such that they are easily settled and established for this style. The natural shoot growth of a jasmine is rather long and whippy, but with the necessary pinching this growth is easily controlled.

Potting. J. nudiflorum is very easily raised by layering and if this method of propagation has been used the young plant should be severed from the parent plant in the autumn, and left undisturbed until early spring. Just before signs of growth appear the young plant is lifted and potted in the chosen container. If it is to be trained in the Cascading style, it is placed a little to one side of the container; if the trunk is to cascade to the right, the plant should be placed slightly to the left of the centre. (See Chapter 5, page 64, for details of training roots to a stone.)

Wiring. The bark of this jasmine is easily damaged by wiring and to avoid this the wire is wound round with narrow strips of paper before applying it to the shoots; subsequent bending of the wired shoots or main trunk has to be done with great caution, as they are also very brittle and snap readily.

Shoot-nipping. Once the framework of the jasmine bonsai has been formed, and this can be accomplished in one season, pinching must be carried out regularly to keep the plant compact and to induce the formation of the flower buds (Fig. 27). Winter pruning can be carried out if necessary; sometimes a well-established jasmine will become rather 'nobbly' and will benefit in appearance from winter pruning. The 'knobs' are caused by the repeated summer pinching. The author knows of a garden jasmine that is clipped yearly in early July, and in January and February it is smothered with the yellow star-like flowers. This wholesale clipping seems to have the same effect as shoot-nipping. The clipping is in fact done by the owner to keep the plant tidy.

Note. The flowers are easily damaged by frost as soon as the colour shows, and to avoid any risk of this the jasmine should be brought indoors as soon as the buds begin to get fat—they will in all probability be brought in at this time as it is only then that a jasmine is of interest. They are naturally most welcome at this time of year as the bright yellow flowers bring the first trace of spring colour.

Wistaria brachybotris makes an attractive bonsai and the long racemes show best when placed on a high stand rather than on a table

27. Showing position of flower buds after pinching secondary growth on *Jasminum nudiflorum*

AZALEAS

These are listed here as azaleas because most people still talk about them as such, although they are now included under *Rhododendron. R. obtusum*, which has magenta-coloured flowers, and *R. serpyllifolium*, with rose-pink flowers, are both naturally dwarf and evergreen, with very small leaves, and flower in April or May.

Style. Azaleas are favourite plants to train in the Gnarled and Clasped-to-Stone styles on account of the flexibility of their stems.

Potting. This is carried out when the cuttings are rooted or when the layered plant has been severed from the parent plant for two to three weeks in the autumn. Repotting in future years is best done after the flowers have faded and in nearly all cases it will be necessary every year. The potting soil should not contain lime or chalk, as azaleas are lime haters. If John Innes compost is being used, a special mixture without the usual chalk should be obtained.

Wiring. The bark of azaleas is easily damaged and the wire used must first be covered with paper to give protection.

Shoot-nipping. When the flowers have withered the shoots are nipped leaving two to three leaves. In order to prevent the specimen becoming too crowded some shoots may be left a little longer, and a few of the weakest may be left completely unpinched; this keeps a balanced look and encourages flower-bud formation. In winter if the plant is too crowded some branches may be removed where necessary, but too much winter pruning will cause the growth of undesirably strong shoots in the following growing season.

All dead flowers must be carefully snipped off.

Watering. Azaleas appreciate frequent syringing in the summer months provided that the sun is not on the foliage. They will do best if kept where the sun does not shine on them in the middle of the day. It has been found that the branches are more pliable if water has been withheld on the day before wiring.

Remember that azaleas are lime haters and if possible rain water should be used if they are grown in a chalky or limy district.

Although the plants are hardy, they should be protected from severe frost as the leaves can be spoilt by being 'scorched' in the frost.

DECIDUOUS TREES

ACER PSEUDOPLATANUS (SYCAMORE)

Sycamore trees produce a heavy crop of seeds each autumn which germinate easily their first spring, and so this will probably be the simplest tree for bonsai beginners to dig up in the wild as a seedling; the seedlings settle in pots very easily indeed. The young leaves are an attractive green and often they colour vividly in the autumn.

Style. The Upright and Oblique styles are the most suitable for sycamores.

Potting. Any potting should be carried out in early spring.

Wiring. All the acers can be wired successfully in early summer, but the very young shoots should not be wired until the bark has hardened as it is easily damaged: for this reason remember to wrap the wire with paper if wiring young shoots.

Shoot-nipping. When shoots have produced five or six leaves they should be cut back with sharp scissors, leaving one or two leaves (Fig. 28).

In late June or early July all the leaves are removed, leaving a quarter of an inch of stalk, and in two or three weeks a new set of smaller, fresher leaves will appear which will be proportionate to the size of the bonsai. This leaf-nipping should only be done if the specimen is strong.

After about two or three years the tree may begin to look a little congested, in which case one should thin out the offending branches, making sure that the cuts are 'clean' and no

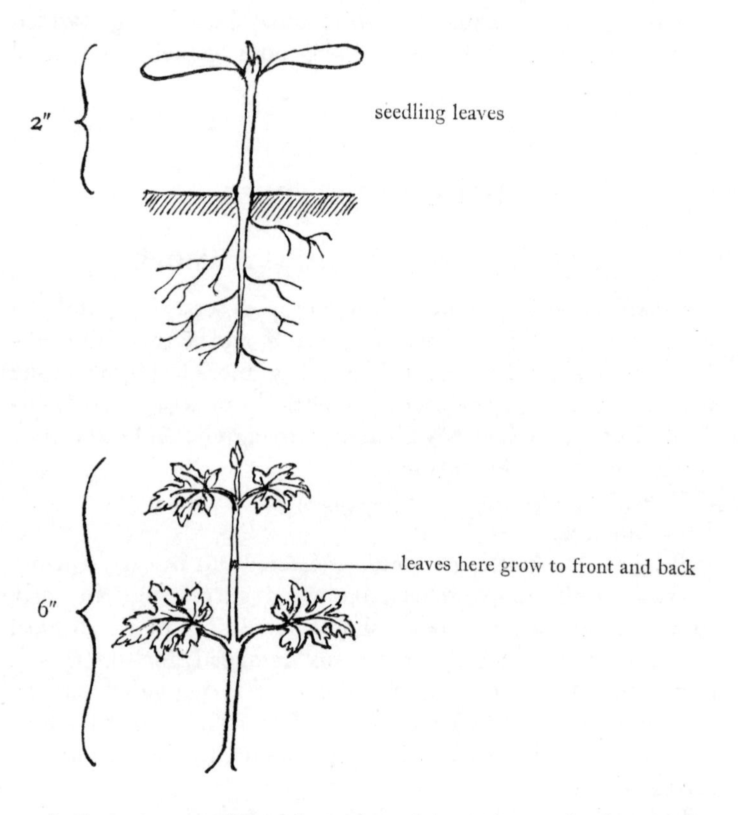

28. Sycamore seedling when planted in spring and a few weeks later ready to have growing point nipped out (see p. 87)

'snags' (pieces of branch) are left; these can look ugly and may possibly rot, often damaging the remaining branches.

BEECH AND SILVER BIRCH

These two trees make very good bonsai, including mame, and the treatment for both is similar. Beech keeps its bronze leaves through the winter and of course trunks of the birch have their own unique silver bark.

Styles. Both beech and birch make admirable Upright and Oblique specimens; they are also suitable for group planting to form wood-like bonsai.

Potting. Seedlings are easily raised by sowing the seed as soon as it is ripe and the resulting seedlings may be potted up when they are well grown, usually twelve to eighteen months after sowing. The best time for potting, however, is in March or April when possible.

If a group planting is being formed the seedlings should be planted in the final container, and odd numbers are easier than even numbers to arrange attractively. Before planting a group of seedlings it is a help to arrange a selection out on the bench or table and study them. Include several taller than the rest to avoid a flat, uninteresting line, and try to plant them in a random arrangement to make the most natural shape possible. Oval or oblong containers are best for group planting (see Fig. 14).

Wiring. Spring and summer are the best times for wiring and in both cases the wire should be wrapped in paper.

Shoot-nipping. When the seedlings have reached the desired height, the tip of the leading shoot should be pinched out. This will encourage the growth of side branches if these have not yet appeared. For the individual specimens a certain proportion of the trunk at the base should be kept free of branches and any that appear should be removed immediately.

All other shoots should be pinched to two or three leaves as soon as the fifth leaf has been formed. Usually this will only need doing to each shoot once in a growing season.

Beech trees will respond well to leaf-trimming if they are strong and vigorous, i.e. the removal of all leaves in late spring.

Watering. Generous watering will be needed in the height of the growing season, but should not be overdone after leaf-trimming the beech. Both beech and birch will stand plenty of sun except in the hottest part of the summer, when a light shade should be provided at midday.

The bark of the birch will need an occasional wash with plain water to keep the silvery surface fresh in appearance.

SALIX BABYLONICA (WEEPING WILLOW)

Style. Weeping willows are best suited to the Cascade style with an oblique trunk, and since the shoots can become as much as three or four feet long, they are shown to their best advantage if raised above eye-level.

First potting. Willows are easily propagated from hard wood cuttings inserted in the open ground in the autumn, preferably at an angle of about 45°. Each cutting should be twelve inches long and inserted for a third of its total length. The buds which will be in the soil must be rubbed off before insertion as well as any unwanted shoots which form on the base of the future stem (Fig. 29).

The cuttings should have formed a good enough root system to put into the selected container in the spring following insertion.

Repotting. Willows are strong growers and will need repotting every spring and often again in the middle of summer. Whenever repotting takes place all the shoots should be cut back to two or three buds. All the soil is shaken off the plant and the roots, which form very quickly, drastically pruned.

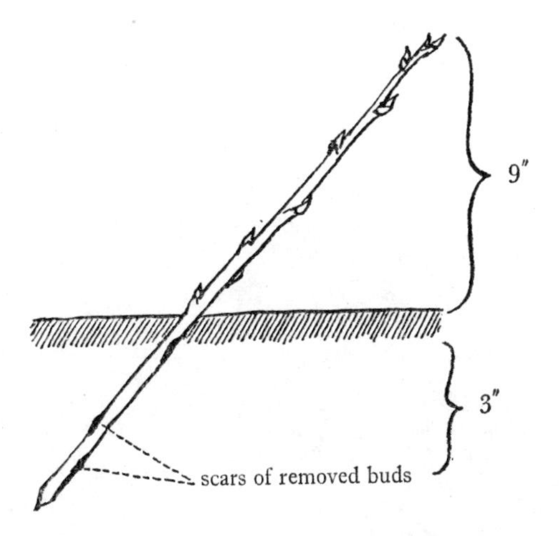

29. *Salix babylonica* (weeping willow) cutting at time of insertion

After repotting in the summer, syringe the plant several times a day and keep in the shade all the time until the secondary growth appears.

Wiring. This should not be necessary.

Shoot-nipping or pruning. In the first summer no pruning or nipping will be necessary except the removal, by rubbing off, of any unwanted shoots. In subsequent growing seasons the previous year's shoots should all be pruned to two or three buds in spring before growth starts. In order to maintain a graceful weeping appearance, it is advisable, where possible, to prune a bud on the lower side of the shoots (Figs. 30, 31).

Watering and feeding. Weeping willows are naturally waterside trees and when trained as bonsai require frequent watering and generous feeding, the latter once a week to prevent the yellowing of leaves in the summer. In very dry weather it is advisable to stand the bonsai container in a bowl of water during the middle of the day.

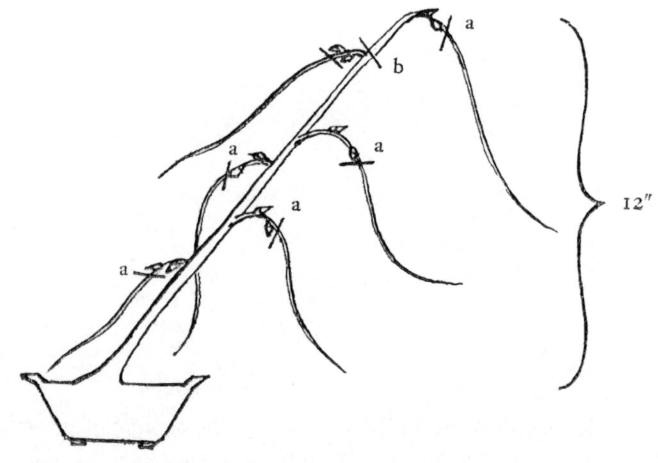

30. First growth of weeping willow pinched at 2nd leaf (a) and tip removed at (b) if the specimen is tall enough (see p. 91)

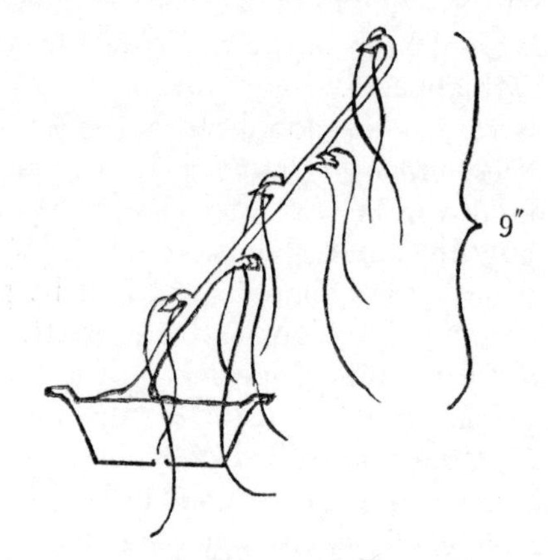

31. Growth resulting from pruning shown in Fig. 30 (see p. 91)

Pinus montana in the Clasped-to-Stone style.
Twelve years old

EVERGREEN TREES

PINUS SYLVESTRIS (SCOTS PINE)

Style. Pinus sylvestris can be trained most effectively in almost all the styles, as in its early years the stem is very flexible and easily shaped when wired. It is, therefore, a good species to train in the Winding style.

Potting. This may be done in autumn or spring.

Wiring. Autumn and winter are the best times for wiring, when the bark has hardened. The newest shoots should not be wired, however, as they are easily damaged.

If the specimen is to be trained in the Winding style, it is necessary to wait until the third or fourth season in order to have a long enough trunk to wire and shape. When wiring is started, the wire is pushed through the soil at the base of the trunk to the bottom of the container (see Fig. 16), and then wound round the base of the trunk, which has previously been protected with a piece of cloth or thin rubber. The first few coils at the base are made fairly close, to hold it really firm, and then continued at quarter-inch intervals for the whole length of the trunk. The trunk is very carefully brought down to a horizontal position and then bent back in the opposite direction below the first branch (see Fig. 17). This process is repeated for the entire length of the trunk and care must be taken to prevent the bends forming immediately above one another. When the trunk has been wired, the branches will be found to be growing at awkward and ugly angles to the trunk. This can be remedied by wiring each one individually and bringing it back to an attractive position; it may be necessary to remove some branches, especially if they hide too much of the trunk.

Sometimes a few of the older needles (those formed two seasons ago) will still be attached to the trunk, and if these are in the way of the wire they may be removed; younger needles, however, must not be pulled off as this action will damage the trunk and bleeding of the resinous sap will be caused. Very often the training of a Winding bonsai can be made easier by tying the bends in the trunk with string after wiring.

Shoot-nipping. The leading shoot may be left unnipped until the bonsai has attained its desired height, when it should be nipped. All other shoots should be nipped when they are about an inch long; the place to nip is just where the needles are beginning to space themselves out and the young shoot stem is showing. Remember not to cut across the needles. If this nipping is done at the right time, it is best done with the finger-nails. This first pinching will cause smaller secondary growths to emerge after four or five weeks, and these are often formed in whorls (all from one place on the trunk). This form of growth is ugly and all shoots from one spot must be removed except one. These secondary growths will probably not need pinching again during the season, but if any of them get much longer than the others they should be removed entirely before the end of the season to maintain the correct balance of the specimen.

When it is necessary to cut into older branches or shoots, the best times are March and September: either before growth starts or after it has finished.

JUNIPERUS CHINENSIS SARGENTII

Juniperus chinensis sargentii makes very attractive bonsai in the Oblique, Cascading and Clasped-to-Stone styles. Quite a pleasing bonsai can be formed in four or five years.

Potting. Rooted cuttings are best potted in the first spring after insertion, and subsequent repotting may be necessary every other year, also in March or April just as growth starts.

Wiring. This can be done at any time of the year except spring.

Shoot-nipping. This should be carried out throughout the growing season and will be most necessary after the first flush of young shoots in late spring, and again in early autumn when the secondary growth is well formed. Any pruning of thicker shoots and branches is best done in the winter.

Watering. All junipers appreciate fairly moist conditions and frequent syringing in hot weather will help the production of a good 'flow' of young shoots.

9
Mame Bonsai

Mame or miniature bonsai could well have more of a place in small houses or flats than the larger forms, as they may be only two to eight or so inches high. On the whole, however, they do not survive to such great ages, mainly because the containers have to be so small, possibly only a little over an inch deep. The containers, as for the larger bonsai, must have a drainage hole and can be of any shape to suit the particular mame bonsai in question (see Chapter 4). The soil mixture, and methods of watering and feeding, are also the same as described in earlier chapters. For obvious reasons, however, they will need watering more frequently, especially in hot, dry weather.

Mame specimens can very often be ready for display in a shorter time than the larger forms, and this in itself is a considerable advantage.

The simpler styles should be chosen for mame bonsai, because their size does not make it possible to train them into the more complicated shapes such as Winding or Clasped-to-Stone. The Upright, Oblique and Cascading styles all make attractive mame bonsai and a group planting can be most effective.

The easiest way to raise mame bonsai quickly is from seed, the best method being to sow the seed direct in the final container. A pinch of seed is sown, as described in Chapter 3, and then thinned out as desired when germination is complete. For a single specimen all the extra seedlings are removed, but for a

Natural seedlings of Holly, Maple and Mountain Ash after potting. The Maple is several years old

Scots pine and Common Spruce seedlings—three years old

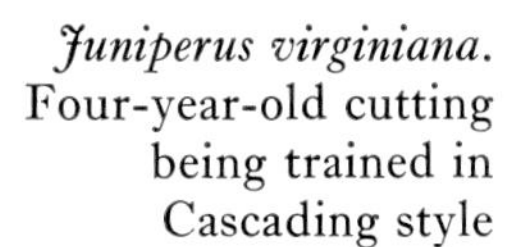

Juniperus virginiana. Four-year-old cutting being trained in Cascading style

group planting two, three or five are left to grow on. In order to avoid too much disturbance in the very small containers when thinning these seedlings, it is best to nip off the surplus seedlings with sharp scissors close to the soil surface. The strongest seedlings should be pinched early in the first season to encourage the growth of side shoots, and if a 'clean' stem is wanted, the lowest of these side shoots must be removed.

Leaf-pinching is particularly valuable as far as mame bonsai are concerned, as it not only corrects any overcrowding and helps to check growth, but also causes smaller leaves to be formed in place of the removed leaves.

Acer, *Pinus* and *Picea* species and *Cryptomeria japonica* all form mame bonsai from seed satisfactorily and of course, if seedlings are obtained, these can be potted up in the spring in the final container. If they are on the tall side, they should be cut back to almost two inches to cause new shoots, one of which is then selected as the leader. If the seedlings have grown very much too tall, the reduction in size should be spread over several seasons.

Three subjects which make good mame bonsai comparatively easily from hardwood cuttings (see page 44) are *Berberis thunbergii* 'Atropurpurea', *Tamarix juniperina* and willows. It may seem strange that such normally large and strong subjects should be recommended for such bonsai, but with careful and judicious pruning and pinching good results can be obtained. When cuttings of four to five inches are well rooted, they should be potted in the final containers. In the spring a suitable wire is wound round the stem, which can then be shaped gradually, usually by bending down; this will naturally have a dwarfing effect. All new growth should be trimmed, almost entirely, early in the growing season to induce more new and dwarf growth. In the case of *Tamarix* this trimming is done after flowering and subsequent growth is left untrimmed, till the dormant season, for flowering in the following year.

When grown from cuttings, Kurume azaleas will also form quite satisfactory flowering mame bonsai after three or four years.

SOME PLANTS SUITABLE FOR MAME BONSAI

DECIDUOUS

Acer See page 26.
Azalea See page 31.
Berberis See page 21.
Cotoneaster See page 22.
Salix See page 30.
Tamarix See page 30.
Zelkova See page 27.

EVERGREEN

Cryptomeria See page 28.
Juniperus See page 28.
Picea See page 28.
Pinus See page 28.

TWO TYPICAL MAME BONSAI SUBJECTS

CRYPTOMERIA JAPONICA

Styles. Cryptomerias have an attractive, neat and upright pyramidal shape, and it is in this natural shape that the mame bonsai will be most successful. In only five years a pleasing and interesting specimen can be formed by starting with a *seed.*

First potting. Propagation by seed is the most satisfactory method of raising a *Cryptomeria* mame bonsai. The seed does not need stratifying (see Chapter 3), and in order to eliminate the risk of damaging the young seedlings it is wise to sow a pinch of seed in the selected container in the spring after harvesting. When the resulting seedlings are established, the strongest and best seedling should be selected and the others removed by cutting off at the soil level.

If the direct sowing method has not been used, a seedling of about five inches in height should be potted in the spring.

Repotting. This is also best carried out in spring as soon as new growth begins to appear, but will only be necessary every three or four years.

Wiring. If wiring is necessary, the wire should be covered with paper to protect the rather soft bark on the young shoots, and should be applied in May when they are at their most flexible stage.

Shoot-nipping. At the time of potting the seedling the leading tip should be nipped out in order to encourage branching; if there are any branches at the time of this first potting, these should be nipped also. Growth will be steady throughout the growing season and pinching must be systematically carried out until growth shows signs of slowing down. Towards the end of the season it is advisable to leave some shoots untrimmed so that the specimen does not have too 'severe' an appearance throughout the winter. At the same time, as it helps to dwarf the specimen this continuous pinching also promotes the formation of young growth which is so pleasing with its fresh green colour. Japanese growers advise the use of fingers only, as the metal of scissors and knives seems to have a detrimental effect on the wound.

Pruning. When the older branches have to be pruned—for example if they are overcrowded or too large—this should be done as growth starts in February or March.

Watering. Cryptomerias appreciate plenty of water and syringing in the summer. To prevent frost 'scorch' or damage some form of light protection should be given in frosty spells; a cold frame would be sufficient.

TAMARIX JUNIPERINA (TAMARISK)

Tamarix juniperina has minute scale-like leaves and plumes of small pink flowers; each plume is about one-and-a-half to two inches long. The tamarisks will be familiar to many people who have seen them growing as quite tall hedges at the seaside; however, when they are subjected to regular pinching, training and root-pruning they can be formed into pleasant little mame bonsai about ten inches tall. When raised from cuttings they will have a quite aged look about them in four to five years only.

Tamarisks flower on the previous season's growth and for this reason *T. juniperina* has been chosen as it flowers in May, thus enabling pinching to be carried out for the first part of the growing season.

Styles. T. juniperina is suitable for the Oblique, Cascading and Clasped-to-Stone styles.

Cuttings. Cuttings about six inches long are inserted in the autumn in a shallow container and left to root in a cold frame, or at least sheltered from extreme cold, until the following spring. The lower 'feathers' are removed from the cuttings.

First potting. In the spring after insertion the rooted cuttings may be potted in the final containers. At the time of potting unwanted shoots are removed either by rubbing with the fingers or with a sharp knife.

Wiring. Using paper-covered wire, one may begin wiring one year after the first potting. The main trunk is wired and trained to the desired shape. Before wiring shorten the branches so as to make a balanced framework to form the bonsai.

Shoot-nipping. Where the branches are overcrowded, shoot removing is carried out as usual until the late spring, when all branches are cut back to the second or third leaf. This will promote secondary growth which is smaller and more in proportion to the mame bonsai. This resulting growth is left untouched until the dormant period, when it is pruned to give a well-shaped specimen. The many flowers will form on this framework.

In subsequent springs the pinching of the early new shoots is carried out up to flowering time and then all growth is cut to two or three leaves as described above.

10
Pests and Diseases

Neither pests nor diseases need loom very large in the mind of a bonsai grower, if all that has gone before in this book has been carried out. If the soil mixture is correct, the watering and feeding carefully administered, and the trees are not kept in too warm or too dry an atmosphere, all should be well. However, both pests and diseases have the habit of appearing with no explanation, except that they have spread from other plants in the garden or neighbourhood, which of course cannot be avoided. It is therefore wise to know what to do should anything adverse appear, and the most common troubles are listed below, together with a recommended treatment.

PESTS

Ants. Little piles of powdery soil appear on the soil surface and under drainage holes. Use proprietary ant killer or water with pyrethrum liquid.

Aphides. These small 'flies' can be black, green or a brownish-red; they suck the sap, thereby damaging the leaves, and also leave on the foliage a sticky substance which encourages the growth of fungal diseases. Spray or dust with malathion or pyrethrum.

Boring insects. These leave a shiny trail on the surface of bark and bore right into the wood, in extreme cases killing a branch or the tree. Fill the holes with D.D.T. dust and seal them with wax or clay.

Earthworms. These can be tiresome and cause disturbance in the roots, especially if the containers have been plunged in the garden. Water with liquid pyrethrum or a proprietary worm killer.

Red spider. These minute red or yellowish mites appear on the underside of leaves of deciduous trees, causing them to become mottled and later yellow; they are particularly a nuisance in dry weather. Frequent syringing (but not in the sun) can do much to prevent attack; spray or dust with malathion.

Scale insects. These look like little brown or whitish shells or bumps mainly on the bark, but sometimes on the foliage; they can be seen at any time of the year. Spray or dust with malathion.

Slugs and snails. Occasional use of slug bait in pellet form placed round the base of containers and on soil surface will control these pests.

DISEASE

Mildew. This fungus appears as powdery patches on the leaves and is encouraged by the 'honeydew' left by aphis attack; the leaves curl and become useless and young shoots gradually wither. Spray with Karathane or another proprietary mildew spray.

OTHER DAMAGE

There are a few other injuries that may damage bonsai and these are of an accidental nature and are not caused by pests or diseases.

Withered leaves. This symptom may be caused by:

1. Lack of water.
2. Too much water.
3. Too strong a food mixture.

Buds dropping. This is usually caused by a lack of water when the buds were forming.

Leaves turning brown. This symptom may also be caused by one of several things:

1. Scorch due to hot sun on wet leaves—usually through glass.
2. If dogs make a habit of 'watering' any plant or tree, it will gradually show signs of 'scorch'.

If leaves or branches do die for any reason, they should be removed carefully with a sharp knife, scissors or secateurs, according to the thickness of the injured part. Sometimes a new shoot can be trained to replace one that has had to be removed, and occasionally the style of the tree may be altered to offset any serious damage.

List of Suppliers

Any list of firms willing to supply suitable plants and containers is bound to be incomplete: there are many nurseries up and down the country which are always willing to help their customers with special requests. The same can be said of potteries. There are numerous pottery firms that welcome personal visits from customers and will even make containers to required measurements.

The author has been in contact with the firms named below but would like to emphasize again that they are by no means the only ones showing a friendly interest in Bonsai work.

PLANTS:

Hillier and Sons,
Winchester.

John Scott and Co.,
The Royal Nurseries,
Merriott,
Crewkerne,
Somerset.

CONTAINERS:

Lotus Pottery,
Stoke Gabriel,
South Devon.

CONTAINERS: (*continued*)

West Meon Pottery,
Doctor's Lane,
West Meon,
Hants.

SEED:

Thompson and Morgan,
Ipswich.

Index